Yankee Doodle
DISCORD

A Walk with Planet Eris
through USA History

Thomas Canfield

ACS Publications
an imprint of Starcrafts LLC

Yankee Doodle Discord
A Walk with Planet Eris through USA History

by Thomas Canfield

First Edition, First Printing 2010

Cover and book design by Maria Kay Simms

Library of Congress Control Number: 2010910144

International Standard Book Number: 978-1-934976-23-4

Published by ACS Publications, an imprint of Starcrafts LLC
334-A Calef Highway
Epping, NH 03042

Printed in The United States of America

DEDICATION

To my parents,
who have managed to live together
for 55+ years without discord.

ACKNOWLEDGEMENTS:

This book could not have been written without the help and support of Maria Simms and Jim Jossick, who channeled Eris in their own way and pushed me to increase the size of the manuscript.

Special thanks need to go to Rique Pottenger, who programmed the course of Eris for the ACS database and included Eris in the ACS ephemerides for the 20th and 21st centuries.

Henry Seltzer (*www.timecycles.com*) must be acknowledged for creating the fine new symbol for Eris, even though some have complained it looks too much like the European symbol for Uranus (Picky! Picky! Picky!)

Nick Fiorenza (*www.lunarplanner.com*) deserves praise for providing graphics of the orbit of Eris.

My thanks, also, to Wolfstar (*www.neptunecafe.com*) for his proposal of the Scorpio rising United States chart that I've found to be the most workable in my own research.

Finally, the editing of the manuscript was done with the generous help of Johonet Carpenter, Meghan Townsend, and Simonne Murphy. (Whatever happens, Simonne, it's not your fault!)

Contents

List of Charts

Foreword

With our publication of *Yankee Doodle Discord,* ACS Publications as an imprint of Starcrafts LLC, introduces what will be one of the first, if not the first, of books to focus on interpretative material for the new planet Eris—technically, a "dwarf planet," but one that precipitated the creation of that new category. When Eris, a planet larger than Pluto, was discovered orbiting beyond astrology's "Dark Lord," astronomers were moved to redefine "planet" in a manner that ultimately stripped Pluto of his full planetary status. Pluto, Eris and Ceres, the largest of the asteroids orbiting between Mars and Jupiter, became the first three "dwarfs."

In the weeks that followed this momentous September 2006 decision of the International Astronomical Union, I doubt if any astrologers, other than strict classicists, seriously contemplated demoting Pluto—certainly not to the point of eliminating him from our charts. I know I didn't! At the time, I was about to send Rique Pottenger's newly updated full 21st century *Michelsen Memorial Edition* of *The New American Ephemeris* to print. Publication was held up while Rique added Eris and Ceres. At the same time, numerous educators played with new little verses with an extra C and E to help school children memorize the order of the planets. Maryn Smith won *National Geographic's* contest with this one: *My Very Exciting Magic Carpet Just Sailed Under Nine Palace Elephants.*

So, like her or not, Eris, named for the Goddess of Discord, is here to stay. Now, how shall we astrologers work with her? How can we get a handle on a planet with an orbit of over 500 years?

Thomas Canfield has taken up the challenge by researching Eris in charts throughout USA history. Why that topic, some may ask, since nearly all USA history to date occurred before anyone knew about Eris? But then the same could be said of revolutionary Uranus, discovered in 1781, *after* the Declaration of Independence that set off the Revolutionary War. Still, Uranus, Neptune (discovered 1846) and Pluto (discovered 1930) are all commonly used by the majority of astrologers in interpreting historical charts.

You'll not find a full analysis of each chart presented in this book. It is about Eris. Of course multiple factors are always in play in any full chart analysis. Indeed, a classical astrologer could likely find a quite satisfactory interpretation of these charts using no planets at all beyond Saturn. Still, through Tom's work, we are shown quite clearly how Eris aspects add supportive nuance to the interpretation of each chart presented, demonstrating a flavor of discord that differs significantly and consistently between soft and hard aspects. In my own tests of Tom's findings on contemporary personal charts, I am seeing that the principle he has discovered works just as well. Our advantage in working with charts for understanding of the present and the future, is that with prior knowledge of how Eris "works," we gain the power of anticipation and the ability to apply personal choice in how we handle our expression of Eris energy.

I am particularly pleased about presenting Tom's book because he is my former astrology student from years past, whom I've now employed as office manager for my reactivation of Astro Computing Services. He is a long-time friend whom I've urged for years to write *something* since I knew he had the talent to do so.

One more thought occurs to me as I complete this Foreword: Uranus has often been touted as quite significant in the USA chart, even though unknown at the birth of the USA. It is interesting to note that Uranus is in a same degree quincunx to Eris on July 4, 1776 (regardless of what exact time on that date might be your preference for the birth chart of the USA). As you will see from reading this book, that Uranus-Eris quincunx can well be considered as a positive reinforcement of the revolutionary energy that birthed the United States of America!

—Maria Kay Simms

Introduction to Eris:
A Hoard of Discord

Meet the Tenth Planet

Who dares to usurp the celestial position of the Lord of the Underworld, and cast aspersions on the discovery of American astronomer, Clyde Tombaugh? Since the discovery of Pluto in 1930, our solar system was considered to be an orderly place with nine planets revolving around the Sun in elliptical orbits. With the coming of the 21st Century, that reliable model has been altered by the discovery of a new planet (slightly larger than Pluto), which would bring into question the qualifications of being a planet, and would even threaten Pluto's standing in the astronomical order. Who dares?

Eris was discovered on October 21, 2003, when the telescope at Palomar Observatory in California recorded its movements. However, computer verification of the sighting did not come until January 5, 2005 in Pasadena, CA at 11:20 am. Credit for the discovery went to Michael Brown, Chad Trujillo, and David Rabinowitz. Due to the size of the new planet, it was possible that there had been sightings earlier, but Eris had not been recognized as a planet. Michael Brown has suggested that even Clyde Tombaugh may have photographed Eris and not known it was a planet. Alas, Tombaugh may have missed the historical opportunity of being the first astronomer to discover two planets in his lifetime.

When the planet was discovered beyond Pluto, its discoverers suggested it be named Xena, after "Xena: Warrior Princess" (Yi Yi Yi Yi!) from the epic TV series. When a small moon was found around the planet, it was named Gabrielle after Xena's sidekick (and possible significant other.) Other astronomers were not happy with planets having the names of fictional TV characters. They preferred classical mythology as the source of planet names. Until they could decide on what name to give the planet, they referred to it by its classification number UB313. Michael Brown also thought of naming it "Lila" which was similar to his daughter's name, Lilah, but those uptight astronomers had to stick with UB313.

Finally, on September 13, 2006, the International Astronomical Union (IAU) decided that the new planet would be named Eris, after the Greek Goddess of Discord. The moon of Eris would be called Dysnomia, after the daughter of Eris, who ruled over a state of lawless behavior. Notice the oblique reference to Lucy Lawless, who had played Xena, Warrior Princess, (Yi Yi Yi Yi!) There was even an element of discord over the presentation of the new planet. When word leaked out about the discovery in the summer of 2005, there were some complaints about why an official announcement was not made. The reason was that Brown, Trujillo, and Rabinowitz had not yet finished their scientific paper on the discovery. Finally, they got with the program and Eris (formerly Xena and UB313) made her debut.

Michael Brown said he was satisfied with the name Eris, because since the discovery the astronomical community had been in discord over the definition of a planet. The IAU put forward a classification of a planet, which said that for a body to be designated as such, it had to have sufficient mass to clear all other bodies out of its orbit. This did not fit Pluto, because Pluto's orbit takes him inside the orbit of Neptune, and puny Pluto has not cleared larger Neptune out of the way. It definitely did not fit Eris, because her long elliptical orbit takes her inside the orbit of Pluto.

Clearly, these orbital oddities would not fit the IAU's vision for a tidy solar system, and there were still plenty of astronomers who considered Pluto to be a planet. Before the end of the 2006 IAU proceedings, astronomers created a new category

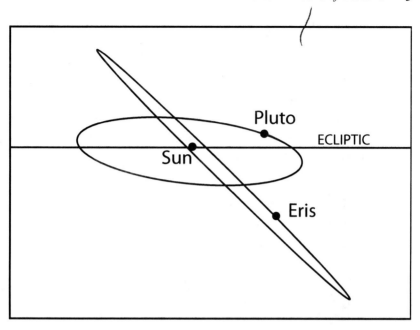

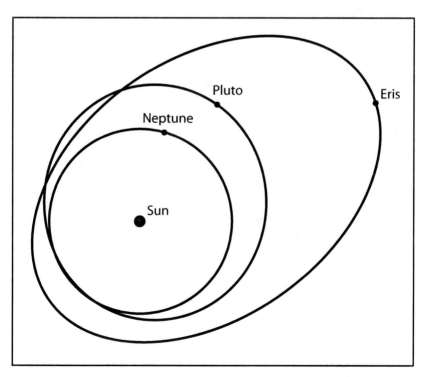

of "dwarf planet", which includes Pluto, Ceres, and Eris. Pluto faced the indignity of being demoted to "dwarf" status, while Ceres experienced a promotion. Originally, Ceres was thought to be a planet because she is spherical in shape, but then she was demoted to the status of "asteroid." Because of the coming of Eris, astronomy books had to be rewritten to the detriment of Pluto and the advancement of Ceres. If Eris would do that with astronomers, what would she do to astrologers?

Eris and Astrology

With Eris as part of the solar system pantheon, a new dimension of astrological study was found, suggesting that it might be workable to use the mythology of the goddess Eris to show elements of discord in a chart. My initial thought was that the worth of Eris might only be seen in the field of Mundane Astrology because her orbit is about 550 years. How could she be judged in a natal chart? Everyone born since 1926 has Eris in Aries. Since powerful nations can last more than 500 years, the course of Eris in history could be studied through her relationship to planetary positions in the natal chart of a nation. An examination of the transits of Eris in a national chart over a period of a few hundred years would help me understand the influence of this new dwarf planet.

With the help of the computer programming of Rique Pottenger, who included Eris in Astro Computing Services' chart calculations, I began tracking the transits of Eris from 1776 to the present, in order to examine how her movement related to the planets in the natal chart of the USA. Because Eris is so slow moving, I used an orb of one degree in looking at the transits. That one-degree orb proved to provide plenty of activity to be studied. For my examination of her natal positions in aspect to other natal planets or angles within the various charts included in my study, I used a maximum four-degree orb.

The Chart of the USA

The most commonly used charts for the USA are set for July 4, 1776 in Philadelphia, PA, though some astrologers are using the

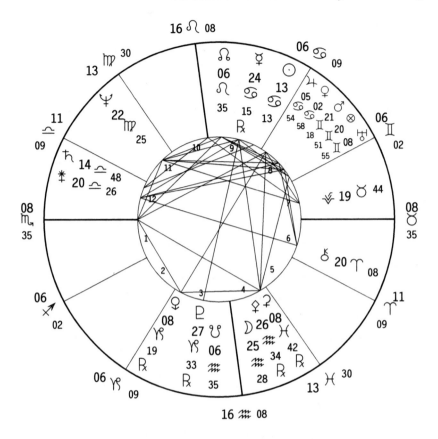

United States of America
July 4, 1776
2:21:00 pm LMT
Philadelphia, PA
39N57'08" 75W09'51"
(chart proposed by Wolfstar)

June 21, 1788 chart for the ratification of the Constitution. There have been many debates over the correct birth time for the USA on July 4, 1776. I prefer using Wolfstar's Scorpio rising chart, because of the interesting Eris aspects to the Ascendant. However, most of the transits of Eris can be applied to the planetary positions of all other USA charts set for the same day, and only the house cusps and Moon positions would vary from chart to chart.

The Eris Frenemy Principle

As I studied the transits of Eris in American History, I came upon an interesting paradox. It was when Eris was in a cooperative aspect (sextile or trine) that Eris exhibited a major discordant influence. When Eris was in a challenging aspect (square, quincunx, or opposition) then the other planet would minimize its influence. I refer to this as the Eris Frenemy Principle, and it fits in with the mythology of Eris. A recent pop culture term, "Frenemy" is an enemy pretending to be your friend for the sake of manipulation, and Eris was the original "Frenemy."

As for conjunctions, the combining of Eris with another planet tends to create a topsy-turvy effect, in which the standard archetypes are turned upside down. Although this can be disconcerting, it is possible for a positive outcome to occur through the upheaval. For example, George Washington had Eris conjunct Mars, and his army was filled with confusion and disorganization, but he still managed to win the war. John Adams had Eris conjunct Mercury, and in spite of his reputation for running off at the mouth, he managed to make sound arguments as a statesman.

According to legend, the Eris talent for discord is in stirring up the pride of individuals, to make them think of their own preeminence, and that their rights and opinions should come first. Such an inflation of ego could lead to murder, or in the case of nations, total warfare. Eris is supposed to enjoy the groans of dying mortals, and her main vacation spot is a bloody battlefield. On a more benign level, Eris can stir up ambition to get people motivated so that they shake off lethargy and start working for their own benefit. Discord comes in when the ambition goes too far.

Although Eris was a Greek deity, she was one of the lesser deities, and certainly not part of the elite group upon Mount Olympus. She was not as powerful nor as attractive as the Olympian gods. However, the greatest influence of Eris came about as a result of her guile and pretended friendship, which provoked jealousy and division. Her most infamous deed was to toss a golden apple into the court of Olympus because she was not invited to the wedding of the sea goddess, Thetis. The golden apple was labeled "For the fairest." The three major goddesses, Hera, Athena, and Aphrodite, all claimed the golden apple, and a major conflict began.

Paris, Prince of Troy, was chosen to decide which goddess was "the fairest." He chose Aphrodite, and was rewarded with the love of Helen, the most beautiful woman in the world. Unfortunately, she was married to the king of Sparta, and when she ran off with Paris to Troy, the Greek kingdoms united for a punitive war against the Trojans. The single act of tossing the golden apple brought about divisions between the Olympian goddesses, and caused the Trojan War, which lasted ten years. If the Trojans could fear the Greeks bearing gifts, the Olympians had more cause to fear Eris and her gifts.

A Glyph for Eris

Astrologer Henry Seltzer created a new symbol for Eris, which looks like the planet Mars, but is pointing downward. This is fitting since Eris is the sister of Ares, God of War, and works with her brother in creating battles.

Mars

Eris

Eris as Co-Ruler of Libra

Author Maria Kay Simms has suggested Eris as a co-ruler of Libra, which fits because Eris can arouse the ego so that personal issues lead to public problems, and cause the Libra scales to go out of balance. This manipulation would represent the dark side of Libra. This would put Eris as a ruler on the opposite side of the zodiac from Mars as ruler of Aries, making a balance between the inspiration and the action (or warmongering and the war.) On the positive side, Eris can instigate change and inspire healthy competition. This can be seen in the charts of some of the leading players of the American Revolution.

The Frenemy Principle in USA History

I first came across the Frenemy Principle when examining the transits of Eris to the USA chart. The first transit of Eris was opposition to the USA Sun in 1782. One would think that an opposition by a planet of discord to the natal Sun of a nation would cause major upheaval. Yet, 1782 was a quiet year, since the Revolutionary War had ended and the United States was here to stay. In 1783, Eris was square the USA Saturn, and one would think that would cause a breakdown in discipline. There was a threat of mutiny, which was suppressed by George Washington, and then he gave up his command and went home. So, there was no discipline discord that year.

I decided to jump ahead to the year 1812, and see what Eris aspects were present for the "Second American Revolution." I was surprised to find that Eris was trine the USA Uranus, which is the planet that rules revolution and upheaval. Now, why would oppositions and squares by Eris be quiet times, and a trine by Eris be a time for war? That was when it hit me, regarding the mythology of Eris, that she causes the most trouble when she is being cooperative but does not cause much trouble when challenged.

In examining the Mundane Astrology of Eris, there could be some discord during the challenging aspects, but it would not be as bad as under the cooperative aspects. For example, the Spanish-American War took place under challenging aspects to the USA chart, but the carnage and destruction for the USA was not as bad as the Civil War, or even the War of 1812, which took place under cooperative aspects. One has to consider the elements of the planets being aspected, and how Eris is interacting with those archetypes. Also, house placement and the nature of each sign should be brought into consideration.

When tracking Eris through USA history, it almost seems as if she were like the dark twin of Forrest Gump, popping up at historical turning points but never being acknowledged for being there. She makes cooperative aspects at battles, attacks and assassinations, befitting the mythology of Eris turning up whenever there is hysteria, fear and uncertainty. At Gettysburg, Pearl Harbor and September 11, 2001, she is offering interesting trines and sextiles. The shooting of Alexander Hamilton and

Abraham Lincoln both have Eris trine Mars. For the assassination of John F. Kennedy, she is conjunct Jupiter and at the focal point of a yod with Uranus and Juno. Her hitherto unknown presence offers an interesting opportunity for astrological re-examination of historical events, and consideration of the Eris Frenemy Principle as an element in the unfolding of circumstances.

The Frenemy Principle in Natal Charts

In regard to the Frenemy Principle, to misquote Shakespeare, some men are born discordant, some achieve discord, and some have discord thrust upon them. Yet, an element of free will does operate in natal charts, even though a person may be living in discordant times. A person's demeanor and attitude to the ego-inflating elements of Eris sometimes helps avoid personal discord. For example, Benjamin Franklin received some of his greatest honors at times of cooperative Eris transits, but rather than let all of this praise go to his head, he managed to keep a humble attitude. John Adams would see discord in his working years, but in his declining years he put forward an attitude of charity and forgiveness, which muted any resentment he might have had under cooperative Eris aspects. Perhaps the best way to deal with cooperative Eris transits is to confront the discord and question how far ambition should go.

In looking at the charts of the Founding Fathers, one can see many more Eris transits to natal planets in their charts than in the charts of leaders born in the 19th and 20th centuries. This is because Eris has a long elliptical orbit, and the speed of the planet was faster during the 18th century. From 1739 on, Eris spent approximately 28 years in Sagittarius, 33 years in Capricorn, 46 years in Aquarius, 80 years in Pisces, and will be spending 124 years in Aries. Because of this current slower transit, Eris is more interesting in the charts of the Founding Fathers, and does not aspect as much in the charts of later generations.

The Eris Discovery Chart

Regarding the chart for the official verification, Eris is in the First House and is retrograde, approaching the Ascendant. After centuries

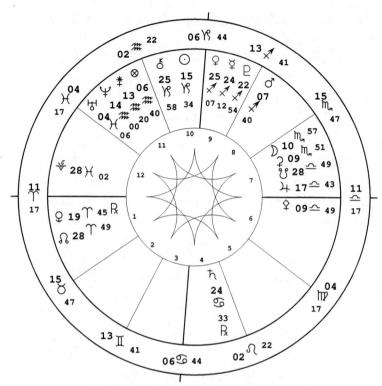

Eris Discovery—Official Verification
January 5, 2005, 11:20 am PST
Pasadena, CA   34N08'52", 118W06'37"

of being unnoticed by astronomers, Eris now has an opportunity to shine. The major aspect Eris makes in the chart is an opposition to Jupiter. Following the Eris Frenemy Principle, it is a time for Eris to accept the Jovian traits of growth and prosperity. Jupiter in Libra is in mutual reception with Venus in Sagittarius, indicating a benevolent attitude as studies go forward. With Venus, Mercury, and Pluto conjunct in the Ninth House of higher education, it may be hoped that there will be courteous and thought-provoking discussion on the new planet, which may bring about some changes in how horoscope interpretations are regarded.

The Midheaven of the Eris Discovery Chart is conjunct the natal position of Eris in the USA chart, and it is with a sense of national pride that this planet, discovered by Americans, should first be examined in the astrological context of American history.

Part I

Eris in Capricorn
Who says a Goat is a Failure?

Author's Note

In my references to Eris moving in time, please understand that whether or not I use the modifier "transiting" each time, I am referring to transiting Eris.

The orb of aspect I have used for Eris in reference to natal charts is within four degrees. For transits of Eris, the orb of aspect used is one degree.

Chapter 1

Eris in the Chart of the USA

With the Eris penchant for pride and pre-eminence, it is fitting that the birth chart of the United States has Eris in the sign of Capricorn. The main issues causing the American Revolution were over finances and control. King George III and Parliament wanted to maintain the right to tax the colonies. The Americans responded with complaints of "No taxation without representation." After the first taxes were protested in the 1760's, most taxes were removed, except the tax on tea. The people of Boston resented the monopoly of the East India Company, backed by the British Crown. Their protest resulted in the most famous tea party in history, with hundreds of cases of tea being dumped into the harbor. This set off a series of events that culminated with independence on July 4, 1776.

At this time, Eris in Capricorn was quincunx Uranus in Gemini. The literature of the Revolution is remembered more than the financial power struggles that caused it. Uranus ruled the spirit of the Revolution, and Gemini gave it the literary power to express the goals of the cause. *Common Sense* by Thomas Paine became the best-selling pamphlet of 1776, and helped convince thousands to join the Patriots. The writings of Jefferson, Adams, and Franklin articulated the themes of liberty, especially in the Declaration of Independence. The documents of the Revolution would be preserved as sacred texts, and made the event seem much nobler than a clash over taxation.

In Wolfstar's Scorpio Rising chart for the USA (page 5 and on the next page for your convenience), Eris is sextile the Ascendant at 8 Scorpio 36. America would present itself as "the land of opportunity" and "a melting pot." These images of transformation would appeal to generations of Europeans and inspire them to make the voyage to the New World. Yet, the discord and the pride of Eris were behind the Scorpio transformation, because competition for jobs and business would be the key to success for the immigrants. The opportunity of America became the need to work harder than your neighbor in order to get ahead. This brutal competition reached its peak in 1861, with Eris at 8 Pisces and trine the Ascendant. Immigrants swelled the population centers of the Northern states and filled the ranks of the Union army during the Civil War. Although there were immigrant success stories, and some remember the immigrants who died in the war, history books do not mention those who worked themselves to death in sweat shops, or fell victim to disease or malnutrition.

In the USA natal chart, Eris is sextile Ceres, the dwarf planet that rules agriculture, animal husbandry, and other nurturing professions. Part of the mythology of the American Revolution involved the warrior farmers, such as George Washington, who left the plow in order to fight. Another part of American mythology is the statesman farmer, like Thomas Jefferson, who left his estate to help govern the nation. Though the idea of the Founding Fathers as simple country farmers was a comforting and idealistic one, the image ran up against hard reality.

With Eris in Capricorn, the icon of the bucolic yeomen was broken by the development of banking interests and manufacturing. Alexander Hamilton's image of America as an industrial power supplanted Jefferson's vision of America as an agrarian nation. The class struggles in America's history involved banks versus farmers, railroads versus farmers, or even the Federal government

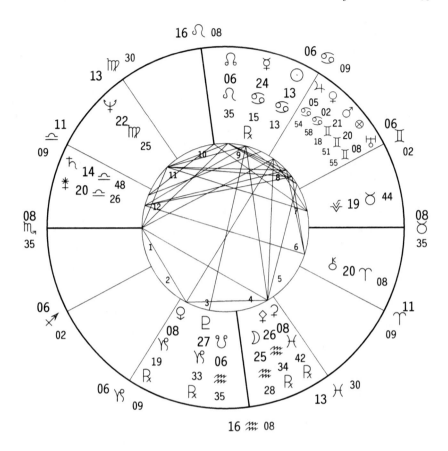

Chart of the USA

versus farmers. Ceres in Pisces lost some of her motherly appeal in this sextile with Eris in Capricorn.

A high point of this Eris/Ceres discord would come in 1861, when transiting Eris would be conjunct the natal Ceres. The industrial Northern states and the agrarian Southern states fought the Civil War that ruined the economy of the South for decades. The Southerners saw themselves as the keepers of the Jeffersonian spirit, and they even saw slavery as a nurturing institution, because slave owners were morally obliged to look after slaves in sickness and old age. Even the abolitionist Harriet Beecher Stowe had to

Shown at right is a photo of an early original sketch for the Great Seal of the United States—an eagle with ancient association to the sign of Scorpio and more dramatic than Benjamin Franklin's original idea of a turkey.

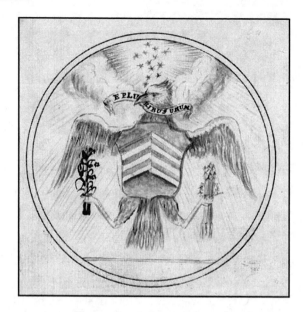

admit in her novel *Uncle Tom's Cabin,* that there were Southerners who were kind to their slaves. The abusive villain of the novel, Simon Legree, was actually a Yankee from Vermont who took a sadistic pleasure in dominating slaves. Southerners contrasted their "peculiar institution" with the conditions of Northern factory workers, who would be left to their own devices by businessmen whose only concern was the amount of profit made. However, there is no record of neglected factory workers selling themselves into slavery for the "benefits."

Eris Marches On

The first aspect of transiting Eris to the USA chart came in 1782 when Eris opposed the USA natal Sun at 13 Cancer 13. Without the Eris Frenemy Principle, one would think that an Eris opposition to a nation's Sun would bring disaster and collapse of the country. However, in 1781 the British defeat at Yorktown broke the resolve of King and country to suppress the new nation. Though final peace would not come until 1783, the battle of Yorktown in 1781 was considered to be the end of the war. From that time on, there was no question that the United States of America would exist as an independent nation. According to some accounts, the

British expressed the discordant feeling at Yorktown by marching out to the tune, *The World Turned Upside Down.*

> *If buttercups buzz'd after the bee,*
> *If boats were on land, churches on sea,*
> *If ponies rode men and if grass ate the cows,*
> *And cats should be chased into holes by the mouse,*
> *If the mamas sold their babies*
> *To the gypsies for half a crown;*
> *If summer were spring and the other way round,*
> *Then all the world would be upside down.*[1]

When Eris opposed the USA Sun, it was a quiet time as the new nation consolidated its power. The major event of 1782 was the creation of the Great Seal of the United States. Since medieval times, a seal was considered to be the symbol of sovereign power. In a time when most people could not read, to have a seal on a document meant that the power of the State would enforce whatever the document said. For Congress to create a Great Seal was a statement that the national power of the United States was a reality.

In 1783, Eris squared the USA Saturn at 14 Libra 48. One might think that this would bring about civil disorders and a breakdown in discipline. This nearly happened at Newburgh, New York, when a group of disgruntled officers threatened to march the Continental Army against Congress to force them to provide back pay for the soldiers. The rebellion was suppressed by the influence of George Washington, who addressed a public meeting and advocated patience, claiming that Congress had not forgotten the needs of the soldiers. In reading a letter from a sympathetic Congressman, Washington had to put on his spectacles, which few had seen him wear. Washington said, "Gentlemen, you will permit me to put on my spectacles, for I have not only grown gray but almost blind in the service of my country." It was a human, sentimental statement, which stirred the emotions of everyone in the room. By the time Washington finished speaking, everyone was supporting him, and the potential rebellion was forgotten.[2]

In 1783, the treaty of peace with Great Britain was signed, officially recognizing the United States of America as a separate nation. The order and discipline of Saturn had held off the discord of Eris. The finest moment of victory took place at Fraunces Tavern in New York City on Dec. 4, 1783 (when Eris was almost exactly square the USA Saturn.) George Washington said farewell to his officers and then departed to return his commission to Congress. Not since Cincinnatus in ancient Rome had a general given up his army to return to his farm. Even King George III was impressed and labeled Washington "the greatest man in the world" for giving up power.[3]

Eris and the Constitution

Though Washington had given up military power, the nation was in need of a central authority as the thirteen states argued amongst themselves as to the rights and privileges each one should have. The drift toward anarchy was made clear in 1787, when a rebellion against changes in the tax code broke out in Western Massachusetts. At the time, Eris was trine the USA Vesta, the asteroid which rules hearth and home. It was feared that the uprising lead by Daniel Shays would start a new revolution. Shays' rebellion was quickly suppressed by the Massachusetts militia. People were once again secure in their property. Yet, the rebellion helped spark the debate over whether a strong central government was needed.

The Constitutional Convention of 1787, presided over by George Washington, managed to put together a document for a new central government that would be ratified by the states. Benjamin Franklin signed the Constitution, not because he thought it was the best possible government, but because he was not entirely convinced that it was the worst. Others who questioned the new powers of the Constitution were mollified by the promise of a "Bill of Rights" to be added later.

The Constitution was ratified by the State of New Hampshire on June 21, 1788, officially becoming the law of the land. Eris was still trine Vesta, and approaching a quincunx with the USA Part of Fortune, a square to the USA Chiron (the wounded healer), and a square to the USA Juno, the asteroid of marriage and partnership.

To this day, there is question as to whether the Constitution provides security for hearth and home, because of the eminent domain clause which allows property to be seized for the public good. Some feared that Americans were signing away their property rights, as typified by Vesta in Taurus. With Eris quincunx the USA Part of Fortune, the ratification of the Constitution proved to be a blessing in dispelling the fears of anarchy. With Eris squaring USA Juno and USA Chiron there was an increase in domestic tranquility, and a healing to the body politic.

On April 30, 1789, George Washington became the first President of the United States under the new Constitution, just as Eris was quincunx the USA Mars. The former general had become the leader of the nation, but he had attained power through electoral means and not through the discord of war. With the USA Mars in Gemini, the only battle Washington faced prior to his inauguration was a protracted debate on what manner of address should be used for the new President. After violent arguments in Congress, in which "Majesty" and "Highness" were rejected, the Congress settled on "His Excellency, the President of the United States."

By 1792, when Eris was trine the USA Neptune, the rise of political parties had begun, with the divided factions promoting fanciful arguments about their rivals. The Democratic-Republican party of Jefferson and Madison accused Washington of wanting to start a monarchy in America, and the wealthy elite was to be a new aristocracy. The Federalist Party of Hamilton and Adams accused the Democratic-Republicans of being too enamored of the French Revolution and declared there was a danger of guillotines being set up in the United States. With the Eris/Neptune trine, this was the beginning of political fantasies that would last for decades.

Another discordant element under the Eris/Neptune trine came about when a group of bond brokers met under a sycamore tree in New York City. They were to form the first stock exchange in the USA, and they would operate out of the Merchants' Coffee House on Wall Street. By the mid-19th century, the brokers of Wall Street would be dominating the economy of the nation, bringing about booms and busts that would enrich and ruin thousands of investors.

In 1794, as Eris opposed the USA Mercury, Washington faced the greatest domestic crisis of his term with the coming of the Whiskey Rebellion. It was ironic that a nation founded by a rebellion against taxation should have to take up arms against farmers in Western Pennsylvania who were violently opposed to the Whiskey Tax. It could have been a struggle that would have damaged the public image and ideals of America. Yet, a major conflict was avoided through communication and negotiation. The power of Mercury suppressed the discord that Eris might have caused.

In 1797, Washington left office and turned the Presidency over to John Adams, just as transiting Eris was conjunct Pluto in the USA chart. The Adams Presidency was marred by international intrigue and mass hysteria at home, represented by the Alien & Sedition Acts. Fears over the French Revolution caused French immigrants to be suspected of being secret agents trying to overturn the American government. Anger against France rose when French diplomats tried to get a bribe from American officials in order to conduct negotiations. The American outrage caused war fever with the cry, "Millions for defense, but not one cent for tribute." George Washington was called out of retirement to help reorganize the American army in case of war.

Some newspaper editors who opposed Federalist policies were imprisoned for sedition, including Benjamin Franklin's grandson, Benjamin Franklin Bache. To be fair to Adams, he was often the victim of lurid and scurrilous newspaper stories. One story claimed that Adams was going to have his son marry a daughter of King George III and return the United States to Great Britain. The alleged plan ended when George Washington, wearing a black uniform, appeared before Adams and told him that another revolution would begin if the marriage took place. Another story claimed that Adams had sent General Charles Pinckney to England to procure four women to be their mistresses. When Adams heard the story, he said, "I do declare upon my honor, if this is true General Pinckney has kept them all for himself and cheated me out of my two."[4]

Thomas Jefferson would later refer to these years of Eris conjunct Pluto as "the Reign of the Witches", because it was a time when the darkest fears of war and subversion brought about the abuse of civil liberties and constitutional rights. Ironically, the greatest subversion was in President Adams' cabinet, with cabinet members who were loyal to Alexander Hamilton giving the Federalist leader confidential reports on plans for war. Fortunately, Adams had the sense to try negotiation one more time. By the time Eris passed into Aquarius, a spirit of accommodation had been reached between the USA and France.

Endnotes:

[1] http://www.contemplator.com/england/worldtur.html

[2] Flexner, James Thomas, *Washington: The Indispensable Man*, New American Library, New York, NY, 1984, 0-462-25542-2, page 174

[3] http://www.cato.org/pub_display.php?pub_id=5593

[4] McCullough, David, *John Adams*, Simon & Schuster, New York, 2001, 0-684-81363-7, page 544

Chapter 2

The Loser of His Country

Natal Discord

In the natal chart of King George III of Great Britain, Eris is conjunct Pallas, the asteroid of Wisdom. According to Maritha Pottenger, "*Pallas is prominent often in therapists, counselors, business consultants, and all kinds of people who relate to others on a more impersonal level, not a committed marriage or living together situation. She also may be key to political action, fighting for social causes, and the entire struggle for equality in the Women's Movement and other groups.*"[1]

With Pallas in the Fourth House, King George III might have had a reputation as a benevolent, fatherly figure. However, with Eris sitting next to Pallas, he is remembered for all the attributes opposite of what Pallas represents. Far from being a "therapist", he is known for being a "madman", and instead of being a "counselor" or "consultant", he is remembered as a "tyrant" and an "oppressor." In American history books, he is the villain, and the King that everyone loves to hate. However, his reign was not a total failure. With Eris squaring his Part of Fortune, the Georgian era became known as a period of prosperity, "the best of times" as Dickens would describe it in *A Tale of Two Cities*. Though the American colonies were lost, Great Britain gained new wealth through domination of India and colonization of Australia and Africa.

With Eris sextile Juno, King George III had to leave a young woman he loved (Lady Sarah Lennox) and take part in an arranged marriage. However, with Eris quincunx Venus, the arranged marriage to Duchess Charlotte of Mecklenburg-Strelitz turned out to be successful, with 15 royal children being born, and the King not seeking any mistresses. As a husband, he was not so much a romantic figure as a man "doing his duty."

With Eris quincunx Neptune, King George III was deeply religious and would spend hours praying each day. He was devoted to the teachings of the Church of England, and would not allow any Roman Catholic emancipation during his lifetime. Even during the Napoleonic wars, he would not allow Roman Catholics to serve in the army. Eris quincunx Saturn reflected a dogmatic and rigid attitude. The King was deeply hurt when his brothers, and later his sons, all took mistresses. His high-handed moralizing drove his sons away and created many fractures in the royal family.

Eris in Sagittarius

The childhood of King George III was restricted and he received private tutoring. With transiting Eris in Sagittarius in the Fifth house trine his Midheaven and opposing his Chiron, the future king received an education that included chemistry, astronomy, physics, mathematics, and agriculture, making him the first English king to study the sciences. How much he learned is questionable, since he was described as being "stupid" and "lethargic", and, according to one historian, "Had he been born in different circumstances it is unlikely he could have earned a living except as an unskilled laborer."[2]

With transiting Eris trine his Mars, he developed an intense hatred of his father, the Prince of Wales, which had difficult consequences in the future. As King George III, he rejected the advice of any nobleman who was friendly to his father, and this included William Pitt the Elder (later the Earl of Chatham) who was the most pro-American figure in British politics and is forever immortalized by the city of Pittsburgh, PA.

The fortunes of the royal child improved in 1752, just after the death of his father. With Eris opposing his natal Sun, he became the Duke of Edinburgh, and was given the title of Prince of Wales.

King George III

His grandfather, King George II, began to lavish attention on him, and political leaders saw him as the coming leader. In 1759, when Eris was square the prince's Vesta, he began his brief relationship with Lady Sarah Lennox, which was broken up by the influence of his domineering mother.

King George III came to the throne in 1760 and married Duchess Charlotte, just as transiting Eris was trine his natal Jupiter, trine his North Node, and sextile his South Node. It was a time of political confusion with the Seven Years War (also known as the French and Indian War in America) continuing. The King's first action was to remove all Whig ministers and replace them with Tory ministers loyal to him. The war came to an end when transiting Eris was opposing the King's natal Mercury and Saturn, bringing hopes of prosperity and a consolidation of British power.

To help cover the expenses of the war, Parliament began issuing taxes on the American colonies, just as Eris was sextile the King's Part of Fortune, and opposing his natal Venus and Neptune. The King and Parliament saw the taxes as legitimate means for raising revenue, but in America the cry of "No taxation without representation" foreshadowed the conflict to come. It was also at this time that the King experienced his first attack of madness, which would afflict him later in his reign.

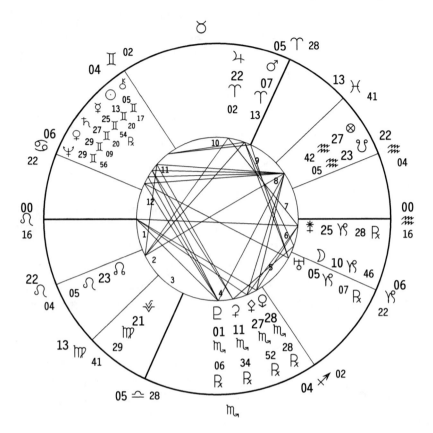

King George III
June 4, 1738
7:30:00 am LMT
St Martin's in the Field, UK
Koch 51N31 0W07

Eris in Capricorn

The negative reaction of the American colonies, while Eris in Capricorn was sextile the King's Pluto, caused a repeal of most of the taxes, except for the tax on tea. The Boston Tea Party took place just as transiting Eris was conjunct King George's Uranus, square his Midheaven, and quincunx his Chiron. There were Americans who were willing to compromise with the King, but his response was to use more repressive measures. Eris was in the King's Sixth

House and squared his Mars in 1775 at the start of armed conflict, in which it was expected Great Britain would win. Transiting Eris would be conjunct King George's Moon in 1778, just as France signed a treaty to support the United States in the war. It was the beginning of the end for British rule over the Colonies. In 1779, with Eris sextile his Ceres, King George browbeat his ministers into continuing the American war, even though they felt it was a lost cause.

The finale came as transiting Eris was quincunx King George's Sun after the battle of Yorktown. Though he lost the American colonies, King George gained his best Prime Minister. The shake-up in the government allowed the King to appoint William Pitt the Younger as his new Minister. At age 24, Pitt was a workaholic who devoted his entire service to the King's interests. For nearly 20 years, Pitt would manage the government with efficiency and diligence, eschewing all marital and social connections for the service of the King.

Eris trined King George's Vesta in 1788, just as he was facing family squabbles with his wastrel sons, and he experienced a major attack of madness (possibly caused by the illness known as Porphyria.) The King was removed from his family and put under the care of doctors for months until they decided that he was well enough to resume his duties. Queen Charlotte would be a major supporter of the King's interests during this time of health crisis.

During the 1790's, when Eris was quincunx King George's Mercury, Saturn, Venus, and Neptune, his reputation began a positive change. His intermittent bouts of madness had aroused public sympathy. The people referred to him as "Farmer George" because of his simple ways and his interest in agriculture. War with France won support for the King as a spirit of patriotism spread over the nation, bringing solidarity of national identity. In 1796, peace overtures with France failed, just as Eris was conjunct King George's Juno. The continuing war caused an increase in taxes, and an outbreak of a Roman Catholic rebellion in Ireland in 1798, while transiting Eris was sextile the King's natal Eris. Although the French aided the Irish rebellion, it was suppressed by British troops. William Pitt advocated reform, but King George III would stand against Catholic emancipation, leading to Pitt's resignation as Eris was leaving Capricorn.

Eris in Aquarius

At the start of the 19th century, Eris moved into Aquarius and entered King George's Seventh House and squared his natal Pluto, bringing about a further transformation of his public image. Instead of being the ruler of separate kingdoms, King George III would be the first ruler of a "United Kingdom." He became reckoned as a force against the spread of the excesses of the French Revolution, and as the main opponent of Napoleon Bonaparte's plans for world domination. When King George III reviewed the troops in London in October 1803, 500,000 people turned out to watch the display. Word was put out that the King was ready to take to the field of battle in the event of an invasion.

King George's political influence began to decline as transiting Eris was sextile his Midheaven and trine his natal Chiron in 1807. The King and Parliament clashed over Roman Catholic recruitment, and after the ministry shake-up the King would no longer take part in political decisions. His illnesses got worse, with cataracts and depression, as transiting Eris was sextile his natal Mars.

In 1811, the Regency was declared with the Prince of Wales managing royal affairs when the King was declared to be insane. The symptoms of madness took the form of hyperactivity, with the King running from one senseless task to another, and speaking non-stop about nonsensical topics for hours on end. Many times he needed to be restrained in a straitjacket. In 1814, with Eris square his Ceres, the Congress of Vienna gave King George the title "King of Hanover", which was mainly a symbolic gesture for him. His wife, Charlotte, died in 1818, as Eris was trine his Sun, but it is unlikely he was aware of the loss. Eris would still be trine his Sun on Christmas, 1819, when he babbled for 58 hours straight. Afterwards, he began to lose control of his limbs, and death would come on January 29, 1820.

Perhaps the most discordant commentary on the shadow existence of King George III supposedly came from the French diplomat, Talleyrand. When told of a rumor that King George III had died, Talleyrand allegedly said, *"There are those who say the King of England is dead. There are those who say the King of England is alive. But I will tell you, in the strictest confidence, that I believe neither!"**

Endnotes:

[1] Pottenger, Maritha, *The Big Four Asteroids: Ceres, Pallas, Juno & Vesta,* An information special provided by Astro Computing Service.

[2] Plumb, J. H., *Our Last King,* American Heritage: The Magazine of History, Vol. XI, No. 4, New York, June 1960, page 95

*Note: The Talleyrand quote came from a book of quotations, and was intended to show that Talleyrand was a cagey character who could not be pinned down. I have not been able to find the book of quotations to list as a reference. Therefore, I can only say the quote "allegedly" came from Talleyrand, though it does match his clever spirit.

Chapter 3

The Foxy Old Man

Natal Discord

Benjamin Franklin was born with Eris conjunct his Juno (the asteroid that rules marriage and partnerships) in the sign of Libra (which is the sign for marriage and partnerships) in his Seventh House (which is the house of marriage and partnerships), and he had the most unconventional married life of the Founding Fathers. He openly acknowledged having an illegitimate son in an age when puritanical morals were still prevalent. His marriage to Deborah Read was a common-law marriage, because she had previously married and her husband had run off with all her money. She received news of her husband's death, but did not receive documentation. Uncertain of her status, she and Franklin declared their marriage before a Justice of the Peace, which was odd for an age when marriages had to be blessed in church. They were a couple until her death in 1774. Franklin would also be known for his risque writings, and for constantly socializing with women in an age where the sexes were usually segregated.

With Eris sextile his natal Pluto in the Fifth House, there were stories that Franklin was a member of the Hell-Fire club, whose members were devoted to orgiastic pleasures. It was certain that he was a Freemason, and one of the leaders of that secret society. It has been revealed that at Franklin's house in London, secret autopsies were done by medical men, and hundreds of human bones were uncovered in the cellar. This was done in an age when medical dissection was a questionable practice, but Franklin was not squeamish about the gross matter of human nature.

Eris was sextile Franklin's Mars in the Ninth House, and most of his legacy was as a travelling diplomat. For years, he represented the interests of Pennsylvania and other colonies in London. During the American Revolution, he made the arguments for independence to the Continental Congress, and then served as America's ambassador to France. His negotiation of an alliance with France, and his efforts in getting supplies and money to America, helped turn the tide of the Revolution.

In Franklin's lifetime, he did not suffer too much during the cooperative Eris transits. Part of this may have been due to a spiritual gift given to him by Cotton Mather. As a young man, Franklin befriended the controversial clergyman. As he was leaving Mather's house, Franklin hit his head on a beam hanging over the doorway. Mather explained that he put the lintel in that position as a reminder to bow and show humility as he left his house. Franklin never forgot that message, and would try to maintain a humble attitude, even as worldly glories were showered upon him.

Eris in Scorpio

When Benjamin Franklin was born in 1706, his father intended that he should enter the clergy. He had two years of formal education, but then his life took a drastic turn at age 10. Franklin's family fell on hard times, and there was not enough money to keep him in school. When Eris in Scorpio was trine his Moon, sextile his Venus, and square his Uranus, he was made a printer's apprentice to his brother, James. During this period, with Eris quincunx his Ascendant, Benjamin began his literary career.

Although Benjamin took an interest in the publishing business, there was no love between him and James. *The New England Courant* was the newspaper printed by James Franklin, and young Benjamin wanted to work as a journalist. When

Benjamin Franklin
January 17, 1706
10:30 am LMT
Boston, MA
Koch 42N21'30"
71W03'37"

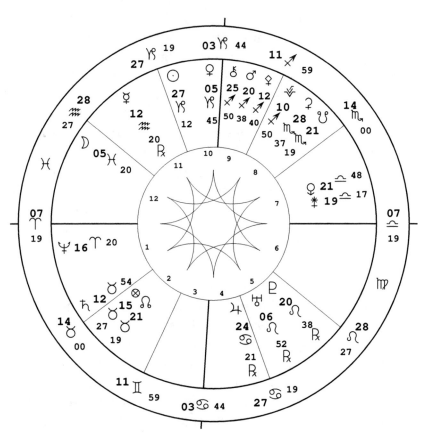

James refused him the chance to write stories, Benjamin tricked his brother by submitting stories under the pen-name of Silence Dogood, a fictional middle-aged widow.

When James found out about Benjamin's trick, he was furious with his brother and forbade him to write any more articles. In 1723, with transiting Eris opposing his Saturn and squaring his Mercury, Benjamin Franklin ran away from his apprenticeship and fled to Philadelphia. This began the fortunes of his career. He worked in various print shops, and was even sent on a mission to England by the Governor of Pennsylvania to buy a printing press. His diligence impressed a wealthy merchant named Thomas Denham, who took Franklin into his business operation.

In 1727, with Eris in Franklin's Eighth House opposing his Part of Fortune, he founded the Junto, a gathering of like-minded businessmen who discussed business conditions and came up with plans to help their companies prosper. Franklin assumed a leadership role in the Philadelphia business community. The Junto began as a discussion group, and then became a book club, with the members sharing books amongst themselves. In 1731, with Eris conjunct Franklin's South Node, and opposing his North Node, he helped found the first public library in America, and he hired the first American librarian, Louis Timothee. This was also the year Franklin's illegitimate son, William, was born, and Benjamin began his common-law marriage to Deborah Read. In spite of these questionable family matters, Franklin also became a Freemason at this time, even though Freemasons were supposed to be of high moral character and not have scandalous relationships in their lives.

In 1733, with Eris trine his Jupiter, Franklin began publication of *Poor Richard's Almanac*, using the pen-name of Richard Saunders. This was the publication that would make him well-known throughout the Colonies. Although it was a regular almanac with agricultural advice and astrological information, the publication was best remembered for the witty aphorisms that Franklin would put into each issue. Although Franklin had borrowed many aphorisms from another author, Lord Halifax, he is well remembered as the creator of the quips.

It was also when Eris was trine Franklin's Jupiter that Deborah gave birth to a son, Francis Folger Franklin. The boy died from smallpox in 1736, when Eris was sextile Franklin's Sun and conjunct his Ceres. Ironically, Franklin was an early advocate for inoculation against smallpox. Benjamin Franklin had intended to have his son inoculated, but he had not gotten around to it.

Eris in Sagittarius

Franklin's only daughter, Sarah, was born in 1743, when Eris in Sagittarius was square his Moon. This was the same year that Franklin first developed an interest in electricity. When Eris was trine Franklin's Ascendant and Uranus in 1746, he was completely immersed in his experiments with electricity, sometimes to the point of nearly electrocuting himself. By 1748, when Eris was conjunct his Vesta, Franklin was one of the wealthiest men in America, and he decided to leave the printing business in order to devote himself to scientific studies.

In 1751, Eris was in Franklin's Ninth House, conjunct his Pallas and quincunx his Saturn, and around this time he may have performed his legendary experiment of flying a kite in a thunderstorm to prove that lightning was electricity. His experiments enabled him to present the world with his most significant invention, the lightning rod, which protected buildings from lightning bolts, and proved to the world that lightning was a natural force and not a sign of divine wrath.

When Eris was trine his Neptune, Franklin attended the Albany Congress in 1754. The meeting was attended by representatives from seven Colonies, and was intended to plan a common defense against the French, and negotiations with the Indian nations. Franklin's main contribution was to offer a plan to unite the Colonies under a central government which would still be loyal to Great Britain. The Colonial legislatures rejected the idea because it meant giving up some of their powers. The proposal was too visionary for its time, but many of Franklin's ideas later became part of the Articles of Confederation.

Franklin spent many years traveling back and forth to Great Britain, representing Colonial interests. In 1759, he visited

Edinburgh, and later said the conversations he had there were "the densest happiness of my life." While Eris was conjunct his Mars, sextile his natal Eris and Juno, and trine his Pluto, he was made an Honorary Doctor of Law by the University of St. Andrews. It was also at this time that he made a major breakthrough with the Penn family, the proprietors of Pennsylvania. He finally got the Penns to agree that they could be taxed by the Pennsylvania legislature. It was also in this year that Franklin came up with one of his wisest quotes, "Those who give up some liberty to attain temporary security deserve neither liberty nor security."

Three years later, when Eris was conjunct Franklin's Chiron and quincunx his Jupiter, Oxford University gave him a doctorate because of his scientific achievements. Keep in mind that in 18th Century England, Americans were looked upon as country bumpkins, satirized by the song "Yankee Doodle." For Franklin to receive doctorates was an acknowledgement that he was the greatest of Americans. With these awards, Franklin had his ego pumped up, and he was afterwards known as "Doctor Franklin." Fortunately, he always maintained a self-deprecating sense of humor to keep his ego from getting too inflated. Yet, lesser mortals, such as John Adams, would later complain about Franklin's sense of self-importance.

Because of his prestige under this transit, Franklin was able to successfully lobby for a new Royal Governor to be appointed for New Jersey. Through his influence, he was able to get his son, William, appointed as Royal Governor, in spite of the stigma of William's illegitimacy. William Franklin would be a diligent servant of the Crown, which would have a sad effect on the relationship with his father in the coming decade.

It was also under this transit, during a return to Pennsylvania, that Benjamin Franklin gained more fame in resistance to the Paxton raids. A mob from the town of Paxton, PA had massacred a tribe of friendly Indians. The mob was heading to Philadelphia to kill Christian Indians who lived near the city. Franklin raised the militia to oppose the Paxton mob, and then he spoke with the mob leaders and convinced them to disperse the mob. Afterwards, Franklin wrote a pamphlet attacking racial prejudice against Indians.

Eris in Capricorn

In 1771, with Eris in Capricorn conjunct his Midheaven, Franklin toured the British Isles, and increased his prestige. Any hope that he could arrange a settlement between the Colonies and Parliament was dashed in 1774 with the Hutchinson scandal. Franklin leaked some letters to the Colonies, which had been written by Massachusetts Governor Thomas Hutchinson. The letters proved that Hutchinson had been advocating repressive measures by the Crown against his own people. With Eris conjunct his Venus and sextile his Moon, Franklin was brought before a committee in Parliament and subjected to all manner of verbal abuse, insult, and ridicule for his part in revealing the letters.

It was at that moment Franklin realized there was no hope of reconciliation between the Colonies and Great Britain. He sailed to America, only to learn that his wife had died shortly before his return. With Eris quincunx his Uranus, Franklin tried to get his son, William, the Royal Governor of New Jersey to support the Patriot cause. William Franklin refused to support his father's politics, and a permanent separation was caused by the issues of the times. With Eris squaring his Ascendant, Franklin began promoting the cause of independence in Congress, leading to the Declaration of Independence, and his role as a diplomat promoting an alliance with France.

Transiting Eris would not aspect Franklin's chart again until 1781, with Eris trine Saturn, marking the end of the war and a decline in his glory days. That year also marked his resignation as Grand Master of the Lodge of the Nine Sisters (referring to the Muses), which was a prominent Masonic Lodge in Paris. Franklin found his diplomatic duties hampered by the presence of obnoxious John Adams, who was sent to help negotiate with Great Britain, but spent a lot of time complaining about Franklin's procedures. Franklin managed to get some peace by having Adams sent off as ambassador to the Netherlands.

In 1785, with Eris trine his Part of Fortune, Franklin returned to America, but retirement was not possible for the 79-year-old diplomat. The State of Pennsylvania elected him as "President" (i.e. Governor) for three years. With Eris square his Neptune, Franklin became a supporter for a new central government. He later became a member of the Constitutional Convention. He realized that the Constitution was not a perfect document, but it had possibilities for improvement. Had Franklin been a younger man, with his prestige, he probably would have been the first President of the United States instead of George Washington.

By 1789, when Eris was trine his North Node, sextile his South Node, and squaring his Juno and natal Eris, Franklin was in declining health and being cared for by his daughter. His last political effort was to sign an anti-slavery document. He died on April 17, 1790, and his funeral was attended by 20,000 people. Franklin looked upon death as both a Deist and a publisher, and once composed his own witty epitaph:

The Body of B. Franklin Printer; Like the Cover of an old Book, Its Contents torn out, And stript of its Lettering and Gilding, Lies here, Food for Worms. But the Work shall not be wholly lost: For it will, as he believ'd, appear once more, In a new & more perfect Edition, Corrected and Amended By the Author.

Chapter 4

General Discord

Natal Discord

In George Washington's natal chart, Eris is exactly conjunct his Mars at 23 Scorpio 14. Discord in martial matters seemed to be a constant problem in Washington's career. In 1775, he was placed in charge of the Continental army, and at once he faced a spirit of chaos. He found an army that was completely disorganized and lacking uniforms, weapons, and even food. He had to deal with constant intrigue, desertions, and threats of mutiny. His retreats were more numerous than his victories. One of the embarrassing topics of the Revolution was that Benedict Arnold won more battles than George Washington. Yet, Washington managed to hold the ragged force together until the end of the war. One can speculate that the real reason Washington did not become a king or a military dictator was because he doubted the competence of the Continental army to sustain him in power.

Eris in Sagittarius

Washington was born in Westmoreland county, Virginia, but at age six, when Eris was quincunx his Chiron, sextile his Midheaven, and trine his Venus, his family moved to Stafford county. Washington was educated at home while Eris in Sagittarius was trine his Part of Fortune and Saturn, and opposing his Ceres. In 1743, his father, Augustine Washington passed away while young George had Eris sextile his Juno. George Washington inherited a small farm, which was managed by his mother until he came of age. At age 14, just when Eris was sextile his Mercury, Washington considered going off to sea to serve as a midshipman in the British navy. His mother prevented that plan from taking place. By 1747, as Eris was conjunct his Uranus, the great influence on his life was his half-brother, Lawrence, who arranged for George to study surveying. George practiced surveying as Eris was quincunx his Pallas. It was a time of discovery for him as he made contacts with Indian tribes, and he developed important social contacts by working for the influential Fairfax family. Washington was appointed to his first public office as surveyor for Culpepper County.

Washington made his only trip overseas in 1751, when he went to Barbados with Lawrence, who was hoping to improve his health. In 1752, when Eris was opposing George's Neptune, Lawrence Washington died from tuberculosis. It was a painful time for George, but he did inherit a large portion of Lawrence's estate, including Mount Vernon, which would become his main estate. One year later, because of his social connections and his knowledge of the wilderness, the Governor of Virginia gave George Washington a commission as an officer, and he left home for his first military adventure.

Washington sparked the French and Indian War in 1754 by attacking a party of Indians who were accompanied by a Frenchman. At first it was thought the Frenchman was a spy, but after he was killed it was discovered that he was a diplomat sent to negotiate with the Governor of Virginia. When Washington constructed Fort Necessity in Pennsylvania for the defense of his men, he made the mistake of building it in a gully, and the attacking Indians were able to shoot down into the fort from nearby high ground. Washington had no choice but to surrender the fort and return to Virginia.

In 1755, when Eris was sextile his Pluto and entering his Eighth House, Washington was under the command of General

George Washington
February 22, 1732
10:00 am LMT
Wakefield, VA
Koch 37N13'21"
76W56'30"

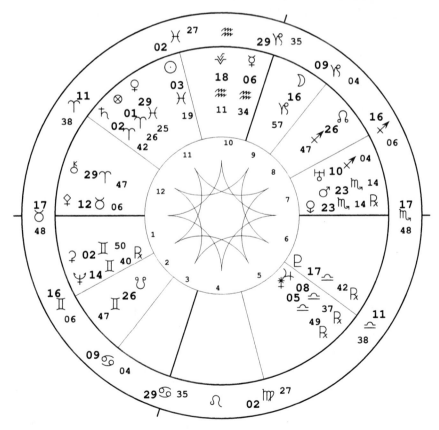

Braddock in the ill-fated attack on Fort Duquesne in Pennsylvania. When the French and Indian surprise attack defeated the British army, Washington helped rally the survivors and lead the retreat. He had two horses shot out from under him, and four bullet holes in his clothing. His successful retreat brought him some military fame, but when Eris was sextile his Vesta he returned to Virginia and did not take part in any further battles during the French and Indian War.

In 1758, Washington became a member of the House of Burgesses, and in 1759 he married the widow Martha Custis. Transiting Eris did not make contacts with his chart until 1765, when it became conjunct his North Node and opposed his South Node. The only major change in his life at the time was that he switched boroughs in the House of Burgesses, representing his own Fairfax County. In 1766, when Eris was squaring his natal Venus and trine his Chiron, he made a decision that improved the economy of Mount Vernon. Instead of producing tobacco as a cash crop, Washington began planting wheat. He found that the edible crop provided sustenance as well as profit for his farm. He started a trend for Southern farmers to consider wheat over tobacco, thereby reducing their dependence on British markets.

Eris in Capricorn

In 1769, when Eris in Capricorn was square Washington's Part of Fortune and Saturn, and quincunx his Ceres, he gained attention by supporting a boycott of British goods in order to protest the taxes levied by Parliament. This boycott caused problems with the British economy, and Parliament removed the taxes, except for the tea tax. The subsequent Boston Tea Party and closing of Boston harbor would bring about the Continental Congress, where Washington served as a delegate from Virginia as Eris was squaring his Juno. This association was the beginning of Washington's rise to power and influence.

According to legend, Washington did not campaign for the position of commander-in-chief, but he did go to Congress wearing his colonel's uniform. When Congress made the offer, Washington accepted the command of the Continental army. By

1776, Eris was square Washington's Jupiter. Although he was commander-in-chief, he had to deal with an impoverished army that had little discipline, and soldiers who would not even dig latrines for sanitation.Washington was often kept busy writing begging letters to state governors, asking for supplies to be sent to the army. In spite of massive British military force, he managed to keep the army together. After retreating across New Jersey he was able to win minor victories at Trenton and Princeton, which improved the morale of the army and the Congress. When Eris entered Washington's Ninth House, the Marquis de Lafayette joined the cause, and the alliance with France gave military aid with the arrival of the French army.

In 1781, with Eris trine his Pallas, Washington was bogged down in various plans to end the stalemate of the war. He kept trying to convince the French to attack New York City to chase out the British, but the French officers realized that it was an impractical scheme. When a chance came to trap the army of General Cornwallis at Yorktown, VA, the French supported that plan. Using the transportation skills he acquired during his retreats, Washington was able to transport the American and French troops from New York to Virginia with great speed. With the French fleet blocking aid from the sea, General Cornwallis was forced to surrender after a brief siege, bringing an end to the Revolutionary War.

In 1783, with Eris quincunx his Neptune, Washington overcame temptations for monarchy or a military dictatorship, resigned his commission, and returned home to Mount Vernon. By 1785, when Eris was conjunct his Moon, trine his Ascendant, and square his Pluto, Washington began to feel uneasy about the political situation with its lack of cooperation between the states under the Articles of Confederation. He had hosted a conference at Mount Vernon for delegates from Virginia, Maryland, Pennsylvania, and Delaware to discuss fishing rights on Chesapeake Bay. The conference did not achieve a resolution, and a follow-up meeting in Annapolis attracted few delegates. Upon hearing about Shays' Rebellion, Washington expressed the opinion that the nation was drifting towards anarchy. He came to realize that a stronger central government was needed, and he was willing to use his prestige to lead the Constitutional convention in 1787.

Unanimously elected President in 1788, Washington was enthusiastically re-elected in 1792. In 1793, when Eris was sextile his Mars and his natal Eris, Washington found himself in the middle of political sniping, which came about as the two political parties started forming. Washington sided mainly with Alexander Hamilton and his Federalist party, and received a lot of newspaper abuse from the Democratic-Republicans, who followed the ideals of Thomas Jefferson. It was partly because of this abuse that Washington decided not to run for a third term.

Washington died on December 14, 1799, just as Eris was conjunct his Midheaven, square his Chiron, and sextile his Venus. The official story was that he died at home after catching a chill. Unofficially, there was a belief that local doctors had bled Washington, and the loss of blood had weakened him so much that he died. After his death, Washington achieved a state of apotheosis, best represented by Brumidi's painting in the rotunda of the U.S. Capitol building. Mythical stories, such as the cherry tree tale told by Parson Weems, would play havoc with the historical facts for a long time.

Chapter 5

Lady Washington

Natal Discord

As the first First Lady, Martha Washington was a source of controversy for the young nation. Some critics accused her of aspiring to monarchy, and putting on airs when she presided over public events. Others said she was appealing to the rabble by opening up receptions to ordinary citizens. Despite the interpretations, she was merely reflecting her upbringing as a Virginian lady, and manifesting the beneficial education that she received.

Born on June 13,1731, Martha Dandridge had Eris in the Second House quincunx her Sun and Mars. Through clear thinking she was able to handle personal difficulties, military problems, and political matters. Whether it was the loss of her children, helping her husband at Valley Forge, or conversing with Congressmen, she was able to withstand all of the difficulties.

Eris in Sagittarius

In 1741, Eris in Sagittarius was conjunct her Uranus, sextile her Moon, quincunx her Mercury, trine her Saturn, and square her Jupiter. Her education was strong on estate management, but weak on grammar and spelling. (In later life, Martha Washington would dictate letters to a secretary, and once the correct grammar and spelling had been put down, she would copy the letters in her own hand.) In spite of the presence of slaves to do the menial work, Martha was instructed in sewing, washing clothes, preparing meals, planting a garden, and preparing folk remedies. With Eris moving into her Third House, she received instruction on etiquette and dancing. Also, she would have learned of the advantages and disadvantages of slavery.

As a teenager with Eris quincunx her South Node, Martha, being knowledgeable about politics, developed a reputation in Williamsburg as the darling of the state legislators. She also became a skilled rider, and according to one story she rode a horse onto the steps of a home. Her most shocking action was her decision to go after Daniel Custis as a husband. He was one of the wealthiest landowners in Virginia, and twenty years older than Martha. Daniel's father was upset by the idea of his son marrying a younger woman, but Daniel went ahead with the ceremony.

By all appearances, it was a fruitful marriage. In 1750, when Martha was married, Eris was sextile her Pluto, and quincunx her Ceres. In 1753, Eris was opposing her Neptune, and quincunx her Venus. Between these years, Martha gave birth to two children, but they did not survive past childhood. She gave birth to two more children, and then her husband passed away in 1757, leaving her to manage one of the largest estates in Virginia.

In 1759, with Eris in Sagittarius approaching an opposition to her Sun and Mars, Martha married George Washington. Historians believe it was not a romantic marriage, but a marriage of business convenience. By marrying Martha Custis, Washington was gaining control of large amounts of property. Martha was gaining a father for her surviving children, as well as a sober and responsible husband. There were no reports of any clash of temperament in their marriage.

By 1764, the only strain on the marriage, when Eris was trine her Pallas, was that the Washingtons realized that they were not going to produce any children. George blamed Martha for the barren condition, and speculated that if she died first, he could marry a young woman and produce heirs. In spite of this attitude, Martha

Martha Washington
June 13, 1731
13:00 LMT
Chestnut Grove, Virginia
Koch 37N41'36"
77W18'06"

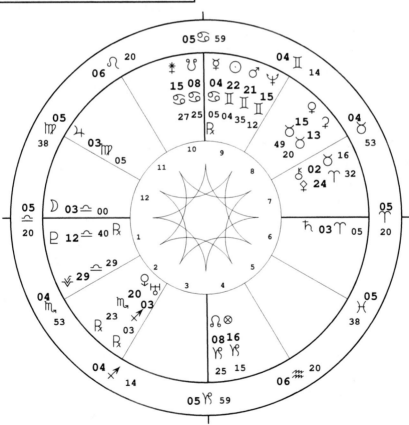

stuck with the marriage. Part of her devotion may have been due to the fact that she was able to use her managerial skills in running the estates. Surviving records show that Martha bought supplies, paid the staff, and took part in decision making regarding the estates. Yet, while Eris was sextile her Vesta, George Washington was making the final decisions about the estate and what crops to plant.

Eris in Capricorn

In 1770, Martha had Eris in Capricorn opposing her Mercury, square her Moon, trine her Jupiter, square her Saturn, and trine her Chiron. It was a time of economic instability between Great Britain and the Colonies, mainly due to a boycott of British goods, sponsored by George Washington. It was a time of shifting loyalties, and changing political images. The people of the Colonies began thinking of themselves as "Americans" rather than just Virginians or New Englanders.

In 1773, with Eris opposing her Midheaven and squaring her Ascendant, Martha lost her only surviving daughter, Patsy. The child had been an epileptic, and had died during a seizure. Martha's only surviving son, John, returned home from college to comfort his mother. It was a painful time for her, but the loss of her daughter gave her the freedom to deal with the arduous tasks she would be called upon to undertake in the years to come.

In 1776, George Washington was commander-in-chief of the American army, and Martha Washington had to face new perils and responsibilities. With Eris in the Fourth House conjunct her North Node and opposing her South Node, Martha took on a stronger persona to deal with the national scene. Some Patriot newspapers suggested that she was a secret Loyalist. Rather than hide behind a demure silence, Martha Washington wrote letters to the newspapers, announcing that she supported the Colonies and her husband in the struggle against Great Britain, and declaring, "My mind is made up; my heart is in the cause." [1]

When the Royal Governor of Virginia threatened to capture Martha and hold her as a war hostage, George Washington insisted that Martha should visit his encampments. She proved to be a valuable helpmate, especially at Valley Forge, and was a welcome presence amongst the generals. She was entrusted with military secrets, and helped George Washington with his correspondence. Martha organized a sewing circle of women to knit blankets and mend the clothing of the soldiers.

Because of her presence, she was widely mentioned in the newspapers, and very favorably, which was a rarity for a woman in 18th century journalism. She also received gifts from notable persons, and had a special gold medal presented to her by her old hometown of Williamsburg, VA. By 1781, as the Revolution was coming to an end, Martha had Eris square Pluto, and she had achieved a fame to rival her husband. She became known as "Lady Washington" and even had a regiment adopt the name of "Lady Washington's Dragoons."

In October, 1781, with Eris trine her Ceres, Martha was to experience her final maternal tragedy. Just as the nation was celebrating the victory at Yorktown, her last surviving child, John Custis, died from typhus fever. George and Martha Washington adopted John's children and raised them at Mount Vernon.

In 1783, with Eris trine her Venus, and quincunx her Neptune, Martha welcomed her husband home to Mount Vernon. It was time to repair the fortunes of the estate which had been neglected during the war, resulting in a $10,000 debt. By 1784, when Eris was conjunct Martha's Part of Fortune and opposing her Juno, Mount Vernon was showing signs of improvement, thanks to George's innovations such as crop rotation and bringing in a flock of sheep for the wool market. George Washington finished the house construction by adding a large two-story dining room, a cupola, and a dove of peace weathervane.

By the late 1780's, the residents of Mount Vernon were disturbed by changing political matters. With Eris sextile her natal Eris, Martha did not want George to become President under the new Constitution, but she had no choice but to accept his decision. She did not attend his inauguration, but traveled to New York at her own pace. The Washingtons lived in New York for a year, until it was decided that the new capital would be moved to Philadelphia.

In 1791, with Eris quincunx her Sun and Mars, Martha settled into the role which later generations would label as "First Lady." Some accused her of following the fashions of monarchy, but her Friday receptions were formal with the intention of establishing respect for the Presidency, particularly among European diplomats. Guests were formally announced. Women would make a curtsey to "Lady Washington", and she would respond with a stiff nod. The reception would end at 9 pm, just in time for the President's bedtime.

By 1794, with Eris squaring her Pallas, Martha Washington was the social leader of the new nation. She was busy making acquaintances and socially grooming future First Ladies, such as Abigail Adams, Elizabeth Monroe, and Dolly Madison. She also began thinking of retirement to Mount Vernon, and accepting the quiet life there. However, she found herself involved with the issue of slavery, when a few of the Washington slaves had run away after serving in Philadelphia.

Eris in Aquarius

After George Washington's death in 1799, when Eris was squaring Martha's Vesta, she assumed control of Mount Vernon. The slaves he owned were given freedom. The slaves owned by Martha were to be given freedom after her death. By 1801, she found herself in the precarious situation of needing to free certain slaves. She could not trust them due to the fact that their freedom would come with her death, and she feared they might hasten her demise. On May 22, 1802, with Eris square her Chiron, and nearing a trine to her Moon, a sextile to her Uranus and Saturn, and a quincunx to her Jupiter, Martha died at Mount Vernon.

Endnote:

[1]Anthony, Carl Sferranza, *First Ladies: The Saga of the President's Wives and their Power 1789-1961,* William Morrow & Co. Inc, New York, 1990, 0-688-11272-2, page 41

Chapter 6
The Confounding Father

Natal Discord

In contrast to Washington's spirit of self-sacrifice, the career of Benedict Arnold was one of self-interest. Yet, the treason that made Arnold into the American Judas might not have happened if he had been given more regard for his accomplishments. Benedict Arnold won more battles than George Washington, and took more wounds for the cause. At the time, his deeds were glossed over, and Arnold was passed over for promotion until Washington himself had to intervene on his behalf. Some historians have pointed out that the Revolution would not have succeeded as well as it had if it had not been for Arnold's early victories.

Eris in Sagittarius

Benedict Arnold came from a prominent Connecticut family, which moved in the best social circles of the colony. His father was a successful merchant, and young Benedict had good prospects. His early years were punctuated with Eris quincunxes to his Jupiter, North Node, Neptune, and Ceres. The only discord at the time was Eris trine his Saturn, which took place the same time as his father's increased drinking.

The first major crisis in young Arnold's life would come in 1756, with the death of two siblings from yellow fever as Eris was conjunct his Venus. (Since his birth time is unknown, we cannot be certain of the house cusps and the Moon position, but the Noon chart places it conjunct Venus, which would fit the family upheaval.) Because of the death of his children, Arnold's father began drinking heavily and his business declined. Benedict Arnold was removed from school to work with his cousins in the apothecary business. He did try to run away and serve in the army, but he was sent home when it was realized how young he was. It was during his brief military service that he witnessed a historical tragedy, later recounted in *The Last of the Mohicans* by James Fennimore Cooper. Fort William Henry had surrendered, and the British soldiers were supposed to have safe passage once they gave up their weapons. Instead, upon leaving the fort they were brutally massacred by the French and Indians. Arnold would never forgive the French for their treachery.

In 1759, Eris was opposing his Chiron when his mother died. In 1761, when Eris was quincunx his Mars, his father died, a broken drunkard, rejected by his church. Arnold was left to care for himself. With the help of his cousins, he thrived in the apothecary business, and went to Europe to buy supplies. In 1764, with Eris sextile his Juno, Arnold formed a shipping partnership, which purchased three ships for trading in the West Indies. Although it seemed a hopeful business venture, profits were cut back by the taxes placed on the colonies by Parliament. Arnold joined the Sons of Liberty, who began agitating against the unjust taxes.

Eris in Capricorn

In 1767, Arnold married his first wife, Margaret, as Eris in Capricorn was in opposition to his Vesta and conjunct his Mercury. The same year Arnold gained notoriety by publicly roughing up a suspected informer. Arnold was fined 50 shillings, but the publicity over the case solidified his reputation with the Sons of Liberty. Through 1770-1771, with Eris conjunct his South Node and opposing his North Node and his Jupiter, Arnold continued his trading voyages, which were essentially smuggling operations.

Benedict Arnold
January 14, 1741
12:00 LMT
Norwich, CT
Koch 41N31'27"
72W04'35"

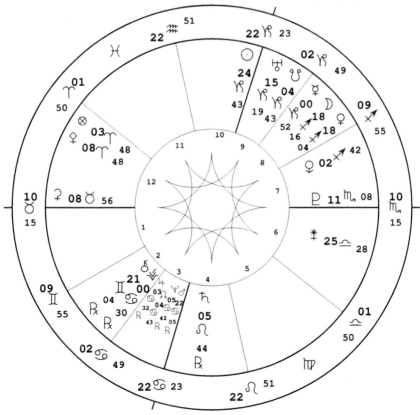

Eris opposing Arnold's Neptune and quincunx his Saturn in 1772 saw the birth of his son, Henry, and an increase in agitation for the Colonial cause. Arnold took a more militant attitude for resistance, and by December, 1774, he was elected captain of the Connecticut militia and ready to take arms against the British.

For most of Arnold's early military career, Eris was square his Pallas and trine his Ceres, during which time he had success on the battlefield, but losses in his personal life. His wife died as he was helping Ethan Allen with the attack on Fort Ticonderoga in 1775. That winter he was part of a failed attempt to invade Canada. He was given command of American forces in Northern New York, and his best success would be at the Battle of Valcour Island on Lake Champlain in October 1776. Arnold supervised the building of a fleet of gunboats, which were destroyed by larger British ships. Yet, the battle delayed the British and made them realize they could not transport troops down Lake Champlain before winter began. The British retreated to Canada to wait for springtime. In 1777, Arnold stopped a British invasion of Connecticut at the Battle of Ridgefield.

In spite of his success against the British, Arnold was the victim of backbiting and bitter politics. He was passed over for promotions, mainly because of the political expediency of promoting other officers first. He was falsely accused of stealing military supplies and was acquitted after an inquiry. Arnold's shipping business had to be sold to cover his expenses. The high tide of his disgust came in 1777 when he played a major part in winning the Battle of Saratoga, but other generals claimed the credit. During the battle he was shot in the leg, and he spent the winter at Valley Forge recovering from his wound and nursing a grudge.

In 1778, Arnold became military governor of Philadelphia, which had been evacuated by the British. There he met and fell in love with Peggy Shippen, the 18-year-old daughter of a Tory judge. When Peggy and Arnold were married in 1779, they began living beyond their means. Arnold attempted to get money through shady schemes, which were exposed and earned him a reprimand from George Washington. After that disappointment, Arnold began listening to his wife's ideas that he should join the

British, with the assistance of an old friend of hers, Major John Andre, an intelligence officer in the British army.

In 1780, with Eris sextile his Pluto, Arnold was involved in the correspondence that brought about the ruin of his life. He attained the command of West Point, and made a deal with the British to surrender the vital area in exchange for 20,000 pounds sterling and a commission in the British army. On September 21, 1780, Major Andre made a secret visit to Arnold to finalize plans, which would also involve the capture of George Washington. HMS Vulture, which transported Andre up the Hudson River, had to withdraw after being fired upon by American batteries. Andre was forced to change clothes and take an overland route back to New York City.

Arnold's plan might have worked if three American soldiers had not captured Andre. The papers of the plan were discovered in Andre's boot. Some of the documents were sent to George Washington, who was on his way to visit West Point. When news came of Andre's capture and that Washington would be receiving the documents, Arnold escaped by rowing down the Hudson River to HMS Vulture, leaving behind Andre to be hanged as a spy. Peggy Arnold was able to use her feminine charm to throw a hysterical fit and convince George Washington that she knew nothing about her husband's plans. Washington was willing to allow Mrs. Arnold to join her husband in New York.

There has been much debate among historians as to Arnold's motivation for treason. Some attribute it to a love of money. Others suggest that it was payback for all the slights he had suffered over the years. One theory was that Arnold hoped to broker a peace between the Americans and the British, returning America to the British Empire under generous terms that would allow the Colonial governments to set the rate of taxation. In recent years, more blame has been put on his Tory wife, and she has been cast as an American Lady Macbeth.

If Arnold was looking for greater appreciation from the British, he was bitterly disappointed. He was made a general in the British army, but at a lower rank than he had in the American army, and he did not receive all of the money he was promised.

He organized British attacks in Virginia and New England, infamously burning the cities of Richmond, Virginia and New London, Connecticut. The British command in New York would not listen to his war plans. After the defeat at Yorktown, Arnold and his family sailed for England so that he could present his plans to the war office. It was during his stay in England that he learned the war was ended.

Benedict Arnold received praise and some money from King George III and Tory aristocrats. However, with the change of government at the end of the war, his presence became an embarrassment to those trying to reach an agreement with the Americans. In 1784, with Eris conjunct his Uranus, Arnold applied for work with the East India Company, but he was rejected with a politely worded letter that suggested his questionable mercenary ways might not fit in with the ethics of the highly mercenary company.

In 1787, the Arnold family (including his sons from his previous marriage), moved to St. John, New Brunswick. Arnold was very unpopular in the community, accused of conducting shady business deals and frivolous lawsuits. When his warehouse burned down, the locals suggested that Arnold had committed arson to get the insurance money. Peggy Arnold managed to escape the unpleasantness by making a trip to the United States to visit her family. Ironically, her Tory family made the transition to accepting republican life in the United States, and her father distinguished himself by becoming Chief Justice of Pennsylvania.

While in Canada, Benedict Arnold performed another act of betrayal by fathering an illegitimate son, whose existence would not be known until after his Last Will and Testament was read. In 1790, with Eris quincunx his Chiron, the locals burned Arnold in effigy, and troops had to be called out to protect the Arnold family from the mob. This action convinced the Arnolds that they should leave Canada and return to England.

When Great Britain went to war with France, Arnold, with Eris opposing his Mars, helped the war effort by outfitting a privateer to prey on French shipping. In 1794, with Eris conjunct his Sun, he began organizing militia forces in the West Indies, and was praised by the landowners for his efforts. He was briefly captured by the French at Guadeloupe, but managed to escape by bribing his guards. In 1796, when Eris was squaring his Juno, Arnold was rewarded with a land grant of 15,000 acres in Canada. However, he did not derive any financial benefit from this gift before his death on June 14, 1801.

As with Washington, there were apocryphal stories about Arnold. One story claimed that just before his death he requested that he be buried wearing his American uniform. Another unsubstantiated story (told to me by a Freemason) claimed that after the Revolution, Arnold made inquiries through the Masonic brotherhood as to whether he would be allowed to return to the United States. The request went all the way to the most prominent Mason in America, George Washington, who turned it down. As much as Washington was glorified, Arnold would be vilified, frequently depicted as a satanic figure associated with those who would betray the nation.

Chapter 7
An Essential Character

Natal Discord

It was John Adams who described his childhood friend, John Hancock, as "an essential character" of the American Revolution. Today, Hancock is mainly remembered for his giant signature on the Declaration of Independence, supposedly written so that King George could read it without putting his glasses on. Hancock's signature was to prove to be vitally essential for the Revolution, since his correspondence and prestige helped motivate the cause. With Eris conjunct his Midheaven, there would be much discord with his business career due to accusations of smuggling, but he would rise above it by taking a political role.

Eris in Sagittarius

Born in Braintree, MA, John Hancock grew up near John Adams, until 1744 when Eris in Sagittarius was sextile his Sun and Ascendant, and opposing his Saturn. Hancock's father died, and young John was taken from his mother and sent to live with a childless uncle and aunt on Beacon Hill in Boston. His uncle was the head of the leading shipping firm in Massachusetts, and young John was put on the fast track to wealth and power. In 1750, with Eris sextile his Mercury and square his Venus, John Hancock graduated from the prestigious Boston Latin School. By 1753, with Eris quincunx his Ceres, he was nearing his graduation from Harvard with a Bachelor of Arts degree.

In 1756, with Eris in his Eleventh House and quincunx his Vesta, Hancock began training for a partnership in his uncle's firm. He became adept at business, and in 1759, with Eris square his North and South Nodes and quincunx his Pallas, he was sent on a business trip to London. During his stay, he attended the coronation of King George III. By 1764, with Eris in opposition to his Neptune, he took over control of the House of Hancock. He entered the legislature, where he became friends with Samuel Adams, an early promoter of Revolution.

Eris in Capricorn

Both Samuel Adams and John Hancock were in the forefront of protest against the taxes put on the Colonies in the 1760's. In 1768, with Eris entering Capricorn and conjunct his Uranus in the Eleventh House and sextile his Pluto in the Ninth House, Hancock's firm was accused of smuggling when Hancock's sailors refused to allow customs officials to check the ships without proper documentation. Hancock was defended in court by his childhood friend, John Adams, and was found not guilty.

By 1771, with Eris sextile his Moon and Part of Fortune, and quincunx his Saturn, John Hancock assumed a leadership position with the Sons of Liberty. The British still considered him to be a smuggler, though no charges could be proven. His reputation grew throughout the Colonies, and his efforts in Massachusetts inspired similar action elsewhere. After the Boston Massacre in 1770, Hancock demanded the removal of British troops from Boston, threatening to lead an army of 10,000 Colonials into the city. The statement made him a marked man by the British who saw him as the rebel leader.

In 1775, with Eris trine his Mars and approaching his Twelfth House, Hancock had a busy year. He was plagued with

John Hancock
January 23, 1737
7:30 am LMT
Braintree, MA
Koch 42N13'20"
71W00'

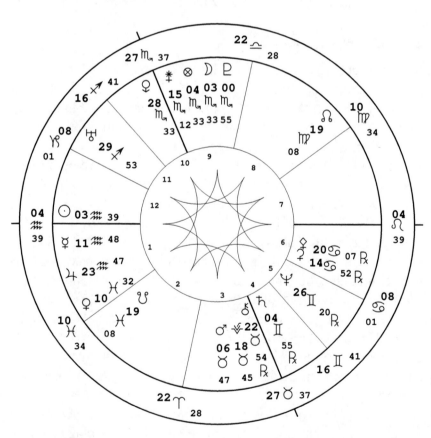

gout, which would remain a chronic condition throughout his life. In April, he had to flee Lexington with Samuel Adams, after receiving a warning from Paul Revere. In May, he was elected as President of the Second Continental Congress. In June, he wanted to be made Commander-in-Chief of the American Army, but was passed over in favor of George Washington. Hancock had to limit his battles to contentious Congressmen debating the issue of Independence, which eventually brought about his famous signature on the Declaration. In August, 1775, he married an attractive young woman named Dorothy Quincy.

In 1778, with Eris sextile his Venus, Hancock had his only military experience, and it proved to be a disaster. Under the command of General John Sullivan, Hancock took charge of 6,000 men, who were to take part in an assault on the British garrison stationed in Newport, RI. A French fleet was to join in the operation, but was damaged by a storm. When French troops did not appear to support the American troops, Hancock's militia suddenly deserted. Hancock received criticism for the desertion, but it did not damage his political reputation.

By 1783, with Eris opposing his Ceres, Hancock was Governor of Massachusetts. He also had to deal with the death of his mother at this time. His leadership style was to take a "hands off" approach and avoid controversial issues. In that sense, he represented the Jeffersonian ideal of "the government governs best that governs the least." His term lasted until 1785, when Eris was sextile his Juno, and he resigned his position because of poor health.

In 1787, with Eris trine his Vesta, Hancock lost his son, George Washington Hancock, who injured his head while ice skating. Hancock was persuaded to return as Governor of Massachusetts, and was re-elected annually until the end of his life. His most important decision was to pardon those persons who had taken part in Shays' Rebellion, an outbreak of mob violence in western Massachusetts against taxation policies.

In 1788, with Eris sextile his South Node, trine his North Node, and opposing his Pallas, Hancock became involved with the national debate on the new Constitution. At first, Hancock opposed the Constitution, but was eventually won over by the promise of having a Bill of Rights added to it. He presided over the Massachusetts Ratification Convention, but did not speak and did not let his views be known until just before the vote, when he gave a resounding speech supporting the Constitution. With wisdom worthy of Pallas Athena, his eloquence was responsible for Massachusetts ratifying the Constitution.

By 1791, when Eris was trine his Chiron, Hancock was in declining health. Even though he served as Governor, he was a figurehead, and did not offer any significant leadership role. He died on October 8, 1793, and was succeeded as governor by his friend, Samuel Adams, who ordered a statewide day of mourning. John Hancock was given one of the largest funerals ever seen in America to that day.

Chapter 8

The Second Bonaparte

Natal Discord

It was Abigail Adams who warned her husband in the late 1790's that Alexander Hamilton was plotting to become a "second Bonaparte." Napoleon had just begun his military career, and his string of victories had made him the man of destiny in Europe. President John Adams came to see that Hamilton was following a similar course in America. Serving George Washington in the raising of an American army to fight France, Hamilton was the guiding force behind the military decisions. President Adams expressed an opinion that Hamilton wanted war with France to get an army raised, which would proclaim a military government with Hamilton at the head of it. Adams would foil this plan by declining to declare war against France, and seeking out negotiation.

There is some uncertainty regarding the birth of Alexander Hamilton in the West Indies. Most historians think it took place in 1755, even though Hamilton once signed a document that declared he was born in 1757. Historians think that Hamilton was trying to shave a few years off his resume. There is no birth time available for Hamilton, which makes it difficult to discuss his Midheaven, Ascendant, and Moon positions. He was born as part of the generation with Eris conjunct Pluto, which would grow up with the impulse to change the world. He also had Eris square Jupiter, which can stand for a struggle between compromise and upholding personal philosophy, in which philosophy might win out. This feature would also show up in the chart of his rival, Thomas Jefferson.

Eris in Capricorn

Hamilton may have been trying to obscure his birth information because of the shame of illegitimacy. His parents were not married and had a stormy relationship. In 1766, with Eris conjunct Hamilton's Mars, his family was abandoned by his father, and his mother had to take up running a store to provide for the family. In 1769, when Eris in Capricorn was conjunct his Mercury, his mother died, and he was adopted by a cousin. In 1770, with Eris squaring his North and South Node, he became a clerk in the shipping firm of Beekman and Cruger in St. Croix, and with Eris conjunct his Chiron in 1771, he actually ran the shipping firm for several months while the owner was at sea.

With Eris trine his Vesta, Hamilton's guardian cousin died, and he and his brother were adopted by separate families. Hamilton was a prodigy with mathematics and grammar, and he wrote articles for the local newspaper. His writing talent was so impressive, the citizens of St. Croix took up a collection to send him to New Jersey for an education. After studying at a grammar school in Elizabethtown, NJ, he entered King's College (now Columbia University) in New York.

In 1775, with Eris quincunx his Neptune, Hamilton published a series of articles supporting the Colonial cause against Great Britain. When war broke out, he joined a volunteer militia group from King's College. He was the leader of a successful raid in capturing British cannons, and afterwards his militia became an artillery company. He was elected captain of the company, and spent much time studying military history.

In 1776, with Eris sextile his Uranus, Hamilton was caught

Alexander Hamilton
January 11, 1755
12:00 LMT
Charlestown, STKN
Koch 17N08   62W37

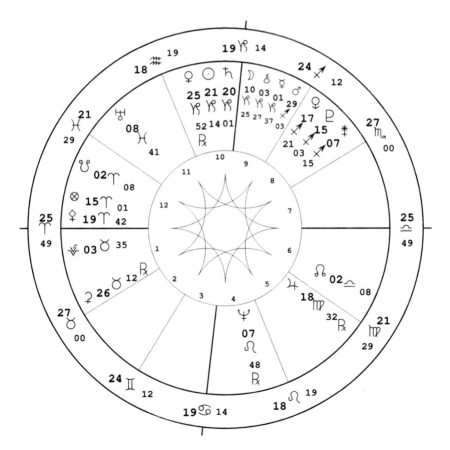

up in the chaos of the invasion of New York. During the retreat from the city, Hamilton planned to launch an attack on a position that had been taken by the British. A young officer brought word that the position had been heavily fortified, and any attack would be suicidal. Hamilton agreed to call off the attack, and admitted that at that moment his life had been saved by Aaron Burr.

During the rest of the Revolution, Eris did not make contacts with Hamilton's natal planets. (This is overlooking the Moon, whose position can not be determined.) Because of his mental clarity, Hamilton was given a position as George Washington's chief of staff, and he handled all correspondence to Congress, state governors, and generals. His greatest contribution was in cleaning up Washington's grammar and spelling errors.

In 1780, he married Elizabeth Schuyler, daughter of General Phillip Schuyler. By marrying into one of the wealthiest families in New York, Hamilton was secure in his future. He risked it all in 1781, by leading an attack in the battle of Yorktown. He ended the Revolution with a record as a war hero and as a friend to powerful and influential men. In the 1780's, he served in Congress, and he became well aware of the weaknesses of the Articles of Confederation.

In 1787, with Eris trine his Jupiter and square his Pallas, Hamilton attended the Constitutional Convention and wrote more than fifty of "The Federalist Papers" to promote the cause of a stronger central government. Although Hamilton contributed much wisdom to the Constitutional cause, he was forced to compromise on some of his political philosophy. Originally, he wanted the President and other government officials to be elected to office for life, though they could be removed for malfeasance. He also wanted state governors to be appointed by the Federal government. These measures were changed by the other members of the Constitutional Convention.

Hamilton signed the Constitution mainly because he thought it was a better solution than the Articles of Confederation. In 1788, with Eris conjunct his Saturn, Hamilton organized the arguments in favor of the Constitution. He was resisted by the Anti-Federalists, who saw a Federal government as new tyranny. James

Madison finally overcame the objections of the Anti-Federalists by promising that a Bill of Rights would be added to the Constitution.

In 1789, Eris was conjunct Hamilton's Sun, and he reached the apex of his career by becoming the first Secretary of the Treasury of the United States. He immediately developed plans for having the Federal government assume the war debt from the Revolution, and to give financial backing to the Continental currency and the notes given to veterans of the Revolution. These actions created unscrupulous speculators, who bought up Continental currency from unsuspecting veterans, and then were able to cash in the full value of the paper money. One of these speculators was James Reynolds, who had been dismissed from the Treasury department because of his shady actions.

With Eris conjunct Hamilton's Sun, his ego clashed with anyone who dared disagree with him. In Washington's cabinet, Hamilton was frequently arguing with Secretary of State Thomas Jefferson, who supported a more limited role for the Federal government. With President Washington listening more to Hamilton, Jefferson felt that he could no longer serve in the government, and he resigned to form his own political faction.

During the 1790's, Hamilton carried on a love affair with Maria Reynolds, the wife of James Reynolds. When Reynolds discovered the affair, he started to blackmail Hamilton, who paid the money and continued seeing Mrs. Reynolds. Information about the affair started to leak out in 1794, when Reynolds was arrested on a counterfeiting charge. He offered details of the affair to opponents of Hamilton, with the suggestion that Hamilton had used public funds to pay the blackmail.

In 1795, with Eris conjunct his Venus, Hamilton resigned as Secretary of the Treasury. He had been investigated by Congress for other matters, and he resented that they would not automatically accept his word. After his resignation, news of the Reynolds affair broke in the newspapers. Hamilton blamed James Monroe for exposing the story, and challenged him to a duel. It was only through the intervention of Aaron Burr that Hamilton was convinced that Monroe was not responsible for the story and the duel was not fought.

Hamilton's response to the scandal was to write a kiss-and-tell pamphlet, admitting to the affair, but denying that any public money had been used to pay off Reynolds. His arguments were so compelling, even his wife forgave him for his affair. However, his political career was publicly ruined, and he had to confine himself to be a figure manipulating events behind the scenes.

In 1796, with Eris trine Hamilton's Ceres, he became involved in a plot to deprive John Adams of the Presidency. He began contacting Federalist members of the Electoral College, who were to vote for John Adams and Thomas Pinckney. Under the rules of the time, the person receiving the most electoral votes became President, and the runner up became Vice-President. Hamilton's scheme was to have the South Carolina electors vote for Jefferson and Pinckney, thereby assuring that Pinckney would get the most electoral votes and become President. However, word of Hamilton's plans leaked out, and the Northern Federalists responded by voting for Adams and Jefferson, thereby insuring that Pinckney would not get enough votes to win.

Although Hamilton was considered to be leader of the Federalist party, he was shut out of the Adams administration. However, there were members of the Adams cabinet who were loyal to Hamilton, and secretly gave him information from cabinet meetings. Through the support of George Washington, Hamilton played a leading role in preparing the U.S. Army during the threat of war with France. When President Adams refused to declare war on France, Hamilton expressed bitter disappointment that he had been deprived of a chance for military glory.

Eris in Aquarius

In 1800, Hamilton played political power-broker once again, when the Electoral College became deadlocked. Thomas Jefferson and his running mate, Aaron Burr, had received the exact number of electoral votes. The election had to be decided by the House of Representatives.Though Hamilton had constantly argued with Jefferson, he had a deep, personal hatred towards Aaron Burr, who mocked Federalist policies and once took away a Senate seat from Hamilton's father-in-law. Hamilton used his influence to

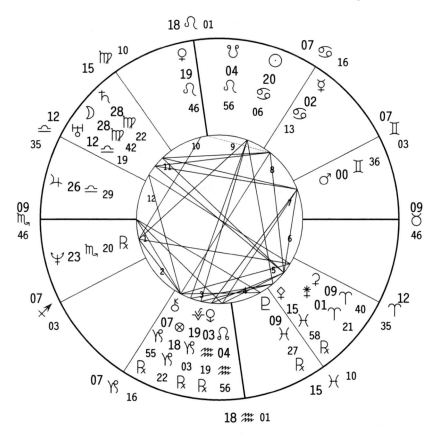

Hamilton's Death
July 12, 1804 2:00pm LMT
New York, NY
Koch 40N42'51" 74W00'23"

have Federalists vote for Jefferson as President.

After 1801, Hamilton returned to New York to practice law and be involved in state politics. When Eris was sextile his South Node and trine his North Node, Hamilton experienced the grief of losing his eldest son, Philip, who was killed in a duel. It was a foreshadowing of the tragedy to come. In the spring of 1804, with Eris squaring his Vesta, Hamilton became involved in a political movement to prevent Aaron Burr from becoming Governor of New York. During his attacks on Burr, Hamilton used the word "despicable" against him. Aaron Burr took that as a personal insult and challenged Hamilton to a duel. When the duel was fought on July 11, 1804, Hamilton fired first and missed Burr. When Burr fired, his shot hit Hamilton in the abdomen.

Hamilton died from the wound the next day. Transiting Eris would mark his passing with a trine to transiting Mars, a sextile to Juno, a quincunx to Mercury, a conjunction to the North Node, and an opposition to the South Node. He would be remembered as an advocate of a strong central government, a promoter of industry and protectionism, and as a victim of the ambitions of Aaron Burr, whose political career would decline as a result of the duel.

Chapter 9

The Wisdom
of the Sphinx

Natal Discord

Thomas Jefferson was born with Eris square Jupiter, and his philosophy became the cornerstone of his existence. Jefferson found it difficult to compromise, though he often had to. He left behind voluminous records of his beliefs, ideas, and inventions, and his political views can be quoted by all parties. Though he was brilliant as a writer, Jefferson was poor as a public speaker, and whenever he was called upon to give a speech he would stammer, stutter, and read in a halting manner. During his Presidency, the only speeches he gave were his two inaugural addresses. As a public figure, he would seem as silent and reclusive as the Sphinx.

Eris in Sagittarius

In 1746, with Eris squaring his Juno, Jefferson's family moved from Shadwell to Tuckahoe, Virginia. His father, Peter Jefferson, had just inherited a property from a deceased friend named William Randolph. Thomas Jefferson spent his formative years amongst the families of his mother's relatives. The Jefferson family would spend seven years in Tuckahoe before moving back to Shadwell. During that time, Jefferson experienced Eris conjunct the Moon, quincunx Chiron, quincunx Neptune, and then transiting into his Eleventh House to quincunx Venus, all without detrimental result.

In 1756, Eris was quincunx his North Node, trine his Mars, and square his Part of Fortune. It was a formative time in Jefferson's education, when he began studying Greek and Latin. He proved to be a brilliant scholar and was able to graduate from William and Mary college at age 19. Jefferson's father died in 1757, while Eris was squaring his Vesta, and Jefferson would later write, "When I recollect that at 14 years of age, the whole care and direction of my self was thrown on my self entirely, without a relation or a friend qualified to advise and guide me, and recollect the various sorts of bad company with which I associated from time to time, I am astonished I did not turn off with some of them, and become as worthless to society as they were."[1]

Starting in 1760, when Eris was trine his Sun, Jefferson spent his time in society at Williamsburg, where influential men advised him to take up the study of law. Jefferson began his legal studies as Eris was square his Mercury in 1765. At the same time, he suffered an emotional blow from the death of his sister, Jane. He experienced a period of depression, which lasted while Eris was trine his Saturn. Jefferson managed to keep active by reading the law with George Wythe, a leading lawyer in Virginia. (Thirty years later, George Wythe would be preparing the legal career of young Henry Clay.) It was also the time when Jefferson made his first visit outside of Virginia, to Maryland and New York.

Eris in Capricorn

By 1769, Jefferson was highly successful as a lawyer, mainly because of the social contacts he had made, and he was involved with 198 legal cases, the peak of his career. It was also the year he entered the House of Burgesses. With Eris in Capricorn conjunct his Ceres, Jefferson began his lifelong project of building Monticello. Though it was to be a stately mansion, Monticello was never to

Thomas Jefferson
April 13, 1743
1:53 am LMT
Shadwell, Virginia
Koch 38N00'46"
78W23'45"

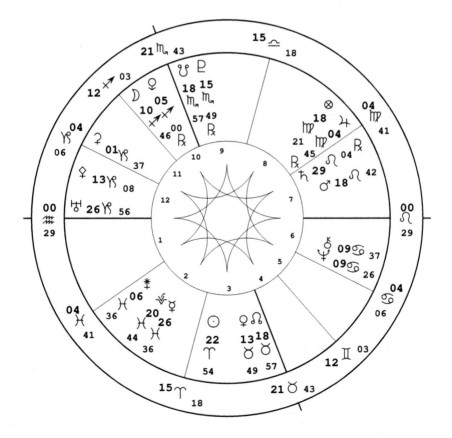

be completed. Over the years, Jefferson would spend a fortune on construction and reconstruction, as he constantly modified and improved his designs. For Jefferson, Monticello was not a home so much as it was a work of art which always needed improvement.

In 1772, when Eris was entering his Twelfth House and trine his Jupiter and Eighth House cusp, Jefferson married a young widow, Martha Wayles Skelton. From a philosophical point of view, it was a successful marriage, with both of the Jeffersons suited to each other in temperament and intellectual skill. However, Martha suffered from chronic ill health, and this would place limits on her ability to travel during their ten years together. The marriage would also bring new slaves to Monticello, including a girl who was the half-sister of Martha, Sally Hemings.

By 1774, with Eris sextile Juno, Jefferson was embroiled in the Colonial cause, and his duties began to take him further away from home. His work *A Summary View of the Rights of British America* aroused great interest and support for resistance in the Colonies. Jefferson was elected to the Continental Congress, and his writing skills brought him to the legendary task of composing the Declaration of Independence. Jefferson left Congress in 1777 to take up a position as a state legislator in Virginia. With Eris opposing his Neptune and Chiron conjunction, it was a time of great activity for him as he began reforming the laws of Virginia. It was also a time when he met and worked with his political protégé, James Madison. Tragedy afflicted his private life as well, when his wife gave birth to a stillborn son.

In 1781, with Eris conjunct Pallas, Jefferson was serving as governor of Virginia. Because of the difficult progress of the war, it was a bleak time in Jefferson's career. Jefferson had moved the capital of Virginia from Williamsburg to Richmond, but British troops under Benedict Arnold invaded Virginia and burned down Richmond. British troops also raided Monticello, and nearly captured Jefferson, who was able to escape in a carriage just before their arrival. This incident would lead to a charge of "cowardice" against Jefferson, and he would be forced to publicly address the matter in Richmond in November, 1782.

In 1782, with Eris trine his Venus, Jefferson lost his

beloved wife Martha. It was an event that sent him into another deep depression, and he was eager to retire from public life. To escape from painful memories, he went to Philadelphia with James Madison for six months. He returned to Monticello in May, 1783, and was prevailed upon to attend the Congress of the Confederation which was meeting in Annapolis. Because of Jefferson's brilliance, he was chosen to be the next ambassador to France to succeed the elderly Benjamin Franklin. (Jefferson's greatest tribute to Franklin was the line, "No one can replace him. I am only his successor.")[2]

In 1784, when Jefferson sailed to France, Eris was sextile his Pluto. It was a difficult time of transition for him. His infant daughter, Lucy Elizabeth, had died and he received word the following year. Jefferson was able to find companionship with the family of John Adams. Abigail Adams and her children had come to Europe to join her husband, who had become the United States Ambassador to Great Britain. As Jefferson prepared his move to Paris, he was frequently in the company of the Adams family as they went shopping and toured the historical sites of France.

Jefferson took up his duties as ambassador to France, just as Eris was trine his North Node, sextile his South Node, and trine his Part of Fortune. It was during this time that he began a relationship with the English artist, Maria Cosway. She managed to fill the emotional void in his life after the death of his wife. Unfortunately, Maria was married, and the relationship could not progress very far because of the threat of scandal. Some historians believe that this was the time that Jefferson started his affair with young Sally Hemings, who had come over to France to be a servant for Jefferson's daughter.

By 1788, with Eris sextile his Vesta, Jefferson was eager to leave France and return to Monticello. James Madison had kept him informed of the new Constitution, and Jefferson was to play a role in the new government that was forming. In 1789, with Eris sextile his Midheaven, Jefferson became America's first Secretary of State. His role in the cabinet was uneasy, because of political conflicts with Alexander Hamilton. When it became obvious that President Washington preferred Hamilton's ideas of government,

Jefferson resigned in 1793 and returned to Monticello.

In 1796, with Eris conjunct his Uranus and sextile his Mercury, Jefferson was ready to return to the political scene. At the time, it would have seemed ungentlemanly for Jefferson to publicly attack Washington, Hamilton, and Adams. So, he paid off newspapers to do it for him. It was said that the abuse from these newspapers were what made Washington decide not to run for a third term. Jefferson came in second in a very close election, and though he became vice-president he found himself shut out of the decision making in the Adams administration.

Eris in Aquarius

By 1800, with Eris conjunct his Ascendant and quincunx his Saturn, Jefferson was in a stronger position to win the election. The Adams administration had grown very unpopular with the Alien & Sedition Acts, which caused the expulsion of foreigners and the arrests of newspaper editors. Still, the election of 1800 was only a narrow victory for Jefferson. In the electoral college, he was tied in votes with his vice-presidential candidate, Aaron Burr, because there was no differentiation between electoral votes cast for a President or a Vice-President. Under the Constitution, the person with the most electoral votes became President, and the person with the second most votes became Vice-President. Because the electoral college could not give a majority, the election had to be decided by the House of Representatives, which was deadlocked between Jefferson and Burr. Although Jefferson expected Burr to step aside, he remained silent, leading Jefferson to suspect that Burr was hoping to become President.

The deadlock was finally broken by Jefferson's old nemesis, Alexander Hamilton, who persuaded a Federalist congressman to vote for Jefferson. Although Hamilton disliked Jefferson, he considered Burr to be totally untrustworthy. Burr was relegated to the ceremonial role of Vice-President, and was not allowed to take part in the decisions of the Jefferson administration. The 12th Amendment of the Constitution was added to make sure that such a deadlock would not take place again by declaring that the electoral votes for President and Vice-President would be counted separately.

Jefferson's first term was free from discord, and considered to be a great success with the purchase of the Louisiana Territory. The Lewis and Clark expedition was sent off to explore the land. Newspaper editors who were imprisoned by Adams were released from jail. One of them, James Callender, became upset when Jefferson would not give him a government position. Callender broke the story about Jefferson's relationship with slave Sally Hemings. Because of Jefferson's popularity, the story was not widely accepted. It was only later when the oral tradition of Jefferson's black descendants was revealed, and a DNA test proved that Jefferson fathered at least one Hemings child, that the Jefferson-Hemings affair officially moved into the history books.

When Jefferson began his second term, Eris was sextile his natal Eris and quincunx his Jupiter. The administration began well with the defeat of the Barbary Coast pirates by Stephen Decatur. Then word came that former Vice-President Aaron Burr was involved in a conspiracy, either to invade Mexico or to cause the western states to leave the Union. Burr was brought to trial on a charge of treason, but released with a verdict of "Not Proven." The conclusion of Jefferson's administration was marred by the Embargo Act, which was a measure to restrict American shipping, to prevent ships from being seized by the warring French and British. It was a measure that nearly wrecked the New England economy, and made Jefferson a very unpopular figure when he left office.

In 1812, when Eris was quincunx his Chiron-Neptune conjunction, Jefferson resumed his friendship with John Adams. Through the intercession of Dr. Benjamin Rush, the former presidents were urged to write to each other. From this began a historic correspondence which lasted more than a dozen years. Historians feel that Jefferson and Adams were not just writing to each other, but to the citizens of the United States, explaining their feelings, their views, and their intentions.

After the War of 1812, with Eris sextile his Moon, Jefferson was in need of money, and he made arrangements to sell his personal library to the government in order to replace the burned Library of Congress. Although he had to part with his beloved books, the money he received was not enough to restore his finances. For the rest of his life, Jefferson would be at the brink of financial collapse, and the selling of land and slaves would not restore his security.

In the 1820's, with Eris square his Venus, and then his Pluto, Jefferson began the project which he hoped would be the crowning achievement of his life. He started work on the University of Virginia, which would be different from the other institutions of higher learning. Taking the design of a Paris hospital, Jefferson built neoclassical pavilions surrounding a lawn with parallel walkways between the buildings. Classrooms were at ground level, and the professors' quarters were on the second floor. Classrooms were kept small to promote air circulation. The buildings were connected by covered walkways, enabling the students and professors to remain dry.

Jefferson's goal was to attract professors away from European universities, and to bring in students from all of the states. The students would pass on what they learned from the European scholars, and a new wave of learning would spread across America. Jefferson wanted the university to have a leading medical school, and he helped design the "Anatomical Theatre" wherein students would learn to perform dissections. He saw to it that the university library was stocked with the finest texts on surgery and pharmacology. Jefferson even had a plan for a state-supported clinic, which would provide health care for those who could not afford it.

By 1825, with Eris quincunx his Part of Fortune, square his North and South Nodes, and opposing his Mars, Jefferson was properly recognized as an elder statesman. The Marquis de Lafayette paid his compliments to Jefferson during his tour of America. As the 50th anniversary of Independence approached, Americans turned to Jefferson for his wisdom. By that time, Jefferson's health was failing, and he was unable to make social appearances. Death came on July 4, 1826, at 12:50 pm, shortly before the death of his old friend, John Adams.

In 2010, Eris was conjunct Thomas Jefferson's Sun, and his name appeared in the news in a discordant manner. The Texas Board of Education voted to remove Thomas Jefferson and his works from textbooks dealing with studies of philosophers from the Age of Enlightenment. The works of Jefferson were to have been replaced with those of Thomas Aquinas (who lived a complete Eris transit before the Age of Enlightenment). There was speculation that Jefferson was removed because he originated the concept of Separation of Church and State. Supporters of Jefferson denounced the decision, and their opposition made the Texas School Board restore Jefferson to the curriculum. As Jefferson wrote in 1804:

> *The firmness with which the people have withstood the late abuses of the press, the discernment they have manifested between truth and falsehood, show that they may be safely trusted to hear everything true and false, and to form a correct judgement between them.*[3]

Endnotes:

[1]   Burstein, Andrew, *The Inner Jefferson,* University Press of Virginia, Charlottesville, VA, 1997, 0-8139-1720-4, page 16.

[2]   Ellis, Joseph J., *American Sphinx: The Character of Thomas Jefferson,* Random House Inc, New York, 1998, 0-679-76441-0. page 91.

[3]   Burstein, page 241.

Chapter 10

"For God's Sake,
John, Sit Down!"

Natal Discord

In the Broadway musical "1776", John Adams makes his entrance, berating the Continental Congress for not debating the issue of Independence. He is rebuffed with a resounding Congressional chorus:

> *Sit down, John*
> > *Sit down, John,*
> > > *For God's sake, John, sit down!*

> *John, you're a bore,*
> > *We've heard this before,*
> > > *Now for God's sake, John, sit down!* [1]

This was a rather appropriate response to someone who had Eris conjunct his natal Mercury in the Third House. For all his life, John Adams would be infamous for his verbiage and his numerous political ideas. Fortunately, his talent for running off at the mouth would be tempered by other elements. Adams had Eris and Mercury in

John Adams
Oct. 30, 1735
2:57 am LMT
Braintree, MA
Koch 42N13'20"
71W00'

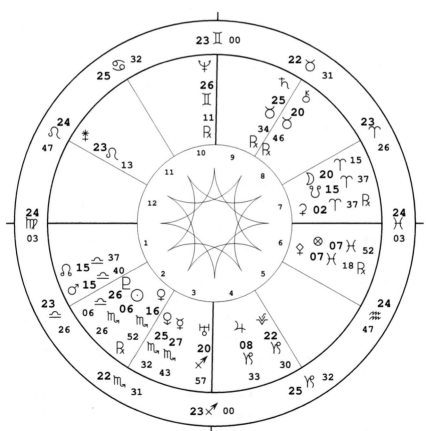

opposition to Saturn, which indicated mental discipline and a structured mind, though some would say that it was too rigid. Eris and Mercury were quincunx Neptune, suggesting religious and moral influences to keep Adams from getting too rambunctious. As Benjamin Franklin once said about John Adams: "He means well for his country, is always an honest man, often a wise one, but sometimes and in some things, absolutely out of his senses." [2]

Eris in Sagittarius

During his childhood, Adams had Eris in Sagittarius trine his Ceres and later square Pallas and his Part of Fortune. The main part of his education was learning about the wisdom of his Puritan forefathers. He came to believe that their principles made them "bearers of freedom", and their cause still had a holy urgency. Adams began thinking of career possibilities beyond the family farm. Although Adams would be involved in farming most of his life, it would only be a secondary interest to him.

In 1753, with Eris sextile his North Node, sextile his Mars, and trine his South Node, Adams was attending Harvard. His studies did not bring any stability to his life. His father had wanted him to become a minister, but Adams did not feel a calling to that profession. While he was making career choices, Adams did some school-teaching in the Worcester area after he graduated from Harvard. Eventually, he came to decide that studying law was the best choice for his career, and he began his studies in the office of James Putnam, a prominent lawyer in Worcester.

By 1759, when Eris was trine his Moon, conjunct his Uranus, and quincunx his Chiron, Adams was admitted to the bar. It was a time of great study for him as he kept important details in his diary regarding legal cases. However, it was also a time of difficulty for him as his father died from influenza in 1761. He would inherit his father's cottage and a small farm, requiring the help of hired men to run it.

In 1762, as Eris was entering his Fourth House, opposing his Midheaven, and squaring his Ascendant, Adams started to take notice of his 17-year-old third cousin, Abigail Smith. She was probably the best educated woman in Massachusetts, receiving a classical education from her father, Rev. William Smith. The relationship between John and Abigail was very cerebral and literary, with both of them writing frequent letters. In 1764, with Eris quincunx his Saturn, John Adams married Abigail Smith and planned for a life of domestic stability.

However, Eris was also trine Juno during the time of their courtship, and the marriage would be plagued by constant separations as John Adams took up work in Congress, and then as an ambassador. Nevertheless, the constant correspondence helped keep a strong bond between John and Abigail, and they would send daily letters filled with news, opinions, and emotional expressions.

Adams found his political voice in 1765 with opposition to the Stamp Act. With Eris sextile his Pluto and opposing his Neptune, he began his career as a revolutionary by writing speeches and articles against the unfair taxation. In December, 1765 he delivered a speech before the Governor and his council, stating the Stamp Act was invalid because Massachusetts, with no representation in Parliament, had not assented to it. Along with his cousin, Samuel Adams, John Adams developed a reputation for powerful ideas on freedom, but it marked him with the British authorities as a troublemaker. King George III would remark, "I have heard of one Mr. Adams, but who is the other?" [3]

Eris in Capricorn

By 1769, Eris in Capricorn was squaring Adams' Ceres, and he moved his family from the farm in Braintree to a rented house in Boston. His increased legal practice required him to be in Boston. He was gaining fame as a lawyer, and he turned down a chance to be an Advocate General for the government of Massachusetts, which he considered to be too Tory. It was also a time for soul-searching for Adams, and his diary reveals that he wrestled with the thoughts that perhaps his political stands were for nothing more than a self-serving desire for fame.

In 1774, when Eris was sextile his Sun, Adams had fame thrust upon him when he was chosen as a delegate to the Continental

Congress. Adams had to leave his family and a thriving legal practice in order to take up residence in Philadelphia. It would mark the end of his life as a private citizen and the beginning of his public life in politics and diplomacy. The First Continental Congress would attempt a reconciliation with Great Britain. When that failed, the Second Continental Congress in 1775 would begin the march towards independence, with John Adams in the lead.

When Adams took part in the Second Continental Congress, Eris was sextile his Pallas and Part of Fortune. It would be a time when he would achieve fame, but his reputation would be marred by the debates in Congress. Although Adams could arrange facts and make eloquent statements, his manner and attitude were repellent to the other members of Congress. Adams developed a reputation for being obnoxious and disliked. Fortunately, the issue of independence had other advocates who could be more diplomatic. Yet, even Thomas Jefferson would credit Adams for having a conspicuous place in the move to independence.

In July, 1776, Eris was conjunct Adams' Jupiter, and he would give the greatest speech of his life in the debate for independence. No record of this speech exists, but those who were present recalled its eloquence and its detail of historical facts. It would be the most successful moment of Adams' life. Ironically, it would be his most deadly moment. Years later, as ambassador to Great Britain, Adams learned that if the British had succeeded and reached a settlement to keep America in the empire, John Adams would have been one of the scapegoats to be hanged to pay for the sins of rebellion.

After the Revolution, Adams would receive the prestigious position of ambassador to Great Britain in 1784, as Eris was square his Mars and his Nodes. He was pleased to be accompanied by his wife and children, providing domestic comfort that he had missed for a decade. The high point of his tenure was to present his credentials to King George III. The "rebel" and "the tyrant" actually got on well together, though Adams would remark that the King's manner of speaking was "odd and strained."

By 1786, when Eris was sextile Adams' Venus, he would find negotiating with the British to be very difficult. There was an underlying animosity towards the Americans, which sometimes appeared in the form of pithy insults in the newspapers. Some of the British took the attitude that sooner or later America would return to the British empire. The government refused to negotiate with Adams on the issues of commerce, debts, and the garrisoning of British troops in America.

Yet, events were taking place in America that would take Adams away from the field of diplomacy. In 1788, a new Constitution was ratified, and many of its features were taken from the Massachusetts Constitution that Adams helped to write in 1779. With Eris square his Moon and trine his Chiron, Adams left the Court of St. James and returned to the United States to take up what he called "the most insignificant office that ever the invention of man contrived or his imagination conceived", namely the Vice-Presidency of the United States. 4

In 1791, with Eris conjunct Adams' Vesta, the Adams family moved to Philadelphia. Residing in a large house called Brushy Hill, they found they had a hard time living within their means, and Abigail complained about the drunken servants. They finally moved to a smaller house on Fourth and Arch Streets. Abigail suffered from rheumatism at this time, and was increasingly feeble due to being bled by the family doctor. It was around this time that political rivalry sprung up between Adams and Thomas Jefferson. While serving in Congress and as diplomats, they had been amiable friends. By the 1790's, Jefferson had made the statement that Adams was guilty of "political heresies." Jefferson attempted to smooth over the ruffled feelings of Adams, but from that time on they began to be seen as rivals.

Adams was re-elected as Vice-President, and returned to office in 1793, when Eris was quincunx both his Midheaven and his Juno. He managed to get some comfort by returning to the family farm in Braintree. He was able to avoid a yellow fever epidemic that raged in Philadelphia from August to November. Adams did not return to Philadelphia until late November once the epidemic had ended.

For years, Adams had been considered as the successor to President Washington, and in 1795 when Washington made his declaration that he would not seek another term in office, people began turning attention to Adams. As Eris was sextile his natal Eris, trine his Saturn, and entering his Fifth House, Adams began dealing with the political rancor that was developing in the 1790's. His greatest opponent was Benjamin Franklin Bache, the grandson of Benjamin Franklin. Bache published a newspaper called "The Aurora", which attacked Adams as "a shameless Monarchist" and referred to him insultingly as "His Rotundity." [5]

In 1796, with Eris squaring his Pluto and quincunx his Neptune, Adams was able to withstand the political attacks from the minions of Jefferson. However, he nearly lost the electoral vote because of the machinations of Alexander Hamilton, who saw himself as the true leader of the Federalists and did not want Adams as President. With the help of his own supporters, Adams managed to win the Presidency by three electoral votes.

Adams began his administration in 1797 with Eris sextile his Mercury, and he received endless abuse from newspapers that were loyal to Jefferson. His position was made more difficult with a crisis involving diplomatic relations with France. Three American representatives in Paris wanted to negotiate with Talleyrand, the French Foreign Minister. They were visited by three French representatives, identified only as "XYZ", who said that Talleyrand would negotiate in exchange for a gratuity. The parsimonious American diplomats scorned the Old World method of diplomacy through bribery.

Many in America became outraged by the incident, and started the cry of "Millions for defense, but not one cent for tribute." Adams and the Federalists increased the military spending, and improved the U.S. Navy for a possible war with France. A "quasi-war" with France began, with American warships attacking French privateers. They also recaptured American ships that had been seized by the French. No formal declaration of war was made against France, although some Federalists like Alexander Hamilton demanded it.

The supporters of Jefferson denounced the "quasi-war" and demanded new negotiations with France. Many newspapers attacked the "pro-British" attitudes of the Adams administration.

In response to these attacks, Adams signed the Alien & Sedition Acts, enabling the government to expel any alien who was considered to be a threat, and to close down any newspaper that wrote against the government. Benjamin Franklin Bache would die while awaiting trial on sedition charges. The acts proved to be so unpopular that more people turned their political support to Jefferson. Adams lost major support in the Federalist party by resuming negotiations with France and averting war. Without popular support, Adams would lose the presidency in 1800.

Eris in Aquarius

Adams returned to his farm in Massachusetts as Eris in Aquarius was sextile his Ceres. He entered a state of personal exile, not communicating with political friends for nearly four years. It was during this transit that Adams was nearly ruined financially. His son, John Quincy Adams, had invested $13,000 of the family savings in a British bank. The bank collapsed, leaving the Adams family nearly bankrupt. John Quincy Adams would sell his own house, use his own savings, and borrow money to buy up the property of his parents' farm so that they would have a secure home.

By 1807, when Eris was square Adams' Sun, he began a correspondence with his old friend, Dr. Benjamin Rush. With this correspondence, he was able to soothe his ruffled ego by explaining his decisions during his administration, and offering his side to history. This correspondence would enable Rush to propose the idea that Adams resume a correspondence with Jefferson. Adams accepted the idea and the historic correspondence resumed in 1812.

Adams was totally immersed in correspondence by 1820 when Eris was trine his Mars and North Node, and sextile his South Node. His beloved wife, Abigail, had passed away in 1818. What remained for him was endless writing and his books. He rarely took part in social events. Constant letter-writing became his main contact with the world, and he went through a spiritual experience that seemed to take the spirit of discord out of his life. Speaking about his correspondence with Jefferson, Adams said, "I forgive all my enemies and hope they may find mercy in Heaven.

Mr. Jefferson and I have grown old and retired from public life. So we are upon our ancient terms of goodwill." 6

In 1824, with Eris square his Venus, Adams was delighted with the news that his son, John Quincy Adams, had been nominated for President. The health of John Adams seemed to rally when his son was inaugurated, but by 1826 his physical and mental abilities were in decline. His last public act, on June 30, was to receive a delegation of town leaders who had come to ask Adams for a toast that could be used on the 50th anniversary of the Declaration of Independence. The response from Adams was "Independence Forever!" When asked for more, Adams replied, "Not a word!"

Endnotes:

1 "Sit Down John," from the 1969 Broadway musical, *1776*. Music and lyrics by Sherman Edwards.

2 McCullough, David, *John Adams*, Simon & Schuster, New York, 2001, 0-684-81363-7, page 285

3 Ibid. page 15
4 Ibid. page 447
5 Ibid. page 462
6 Ibid. page 632
7 Ibid. page 645

Part II

Eris in Aquarius

A Bearer of Troubled Waters

When Thomas Jefferson became President, he faced a potential crisis when Spain ceded control of the Louisiana Territory to France. There was a fear that France would cut off trade with the Americans who shipped their produce down the Mississippi to New Orleans. As Eris was quincunx the USA Venus, Jefferson dispatched Robert Livingston to Paris to negotiate the purchase of New Orleans. To everyone's surprise, Napoleon Bonaparte was willing to sell the entire Louisiana Territory. A deal was quickly concluded which doubled the size of the United States. It was one of the best real estate purchases in American history, with the peaceful influence of Venus negating any discord from Eris.

Yet, in a few years, there would be difficulty with both France and Great Britain. Though America was supposed to be neutral in the Napoleonic wars, each side preyed upon American merchant ships and seized cargo. The British were also seizing sailors from the ships, primarily those who had been born in England. Their justification was, "Once an Englishman, always an Englishman." Jefferson's response to this was to sign the Embargo Act, just as Eris was quincunx the USA Jupiter. For a year, ships were not allowed to trade abroad, and the shipping industry (especially in New England) suffered. Yet, one benefit of the Embargo Act was to increase the amount of American production, especially in textiles, rather than be reliant on other nations for goods. Jupiter, planet of prosperity and growth, managed to lessen the discord from Eris.

The Embargo Act was difficult to enforce, and it was replaced by the Non-Intercourse Act, as Eris was conjunct the South Node and opposing the North Node. Ships were allowed to trade with nations that were not involved in the Napoleonic wars. However, there were still problems with American sailors being seized by the British.

It was a time of discord not only over the loss of material goods, but over the values of the American Revolution as well. There was a willingness to fight to keep King George III from enslaving sailors taken from American ships. There were also fancies about capturing Canada and adding that territory to the United States. Then there was a worry about a British-Indian alliance that would

A View of the Bombardment of Fort McHenry

establish a Native American confederation on the western borders of the United States. This belief was confirmed after the Battle of Tippecanoe in 1811, when the forces of Tecumseh were broken, and Tecumseh fled to Canada to work with the British.

The Star-Spangled Banner

In 1812, Eris was trine the USA Uranus, as well as squaring the Ascendant. There arose a demand for a war against Great Britain that would be a "Second American Revolution." It was a war that did not need to be fought, because Parliament had agreed to ban the impressment of American sailors just a few days before the war was declared. Although the war was fought with revolutionary spirit, the New England states refused to participate in the struggle. Attempts to conquer Canada were beaten back. The British Navy prepared a series of punitive raids against American cities, first burning Washington D.C. in retaliation for the burning of York, Ontario.

After the humiliating destruction of the capital, the people of Baltimore knew that their city would be attacked next. Unlike Washington D.C., which had minimal defenses, Baltimore was prepared for the battle, with militia entrenched outside the city, and ships sunk in the harbor to block the British fleet from sailing in. The centerpiece of American defense was star-shaped Fort McHenry, which withstood the Royal Navy attack for 25 hours on September 13, 1814, ending by the dawn's early light on September 14, 1814.

The battle had been furious, with cannon barrages and Congreve rockets blasting at the fort. When the American soldiers lowered the battle flag in the morning, the British expected they were surrendering. Instead of a white flag, the Americans raised a huge (30 feet by 42 feet) Stars and Stripes flag, signaling that they were not defeated. The British ships withdrew from the battle. Francis Scott Key, an American lawyer being detained on a British ship, was so inspired by the event that he sat down and began writing a poem, "The Star-Spangled Banner," which (in 1931) would become the national anthem.

The chart for 6 am on September 14, 1814, when Key was composing his work, has Eris in the Fifth House. This may symbolize the musical discord that has come from the work, since it was set to the tune of "Anacreon in Heaven", an English drinking song, with a range of high and low notes. It would take singers with almost operatic voices to be able to sing the anthem without missing a note.

In the chart of the "Star-Spangled Banner", there is a stellium in the Twelfth House of hidden matters. With the Sun, Jupiter, Mars, and Mercury conjunct, there were elements for a significant victory. Before the dawn, there was doubt as to whether Fort McHenry would be able to continue the battle, and the darkness added to the fears of surrender. With the arrival of the Sun in the Twelfth House and the inspiring image of the giant flag, all doubts were removed.

Eris in the Fifth House is quincunx Juno in the Twelfth House, and Key's creative work would mark a marriage of music and patriotism. With Eris squaring Pallas in the Eighth House, the song would also represent the standard for military glory. "The Star-Spangled Banner" would be a constant reminder of endurance in times of peril, and a spirit of determination even when the outcome is uncertain, which would fit in with its performances at sporting events.

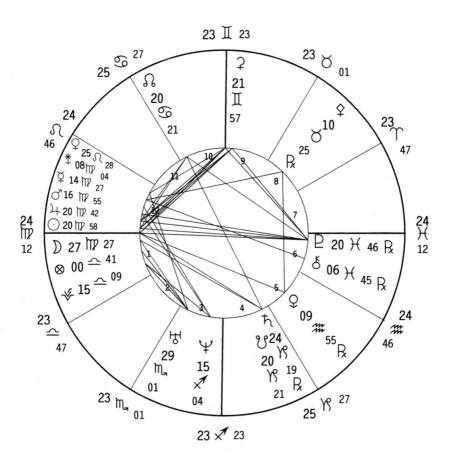

Star Spangled Banner
September 14, 1814
6:00 am LMT, Baltimore, MD
Koch 39N17'25" 76W36'46"

    In 1815, the last British invasion for the seizure of New Orleans was defeated by General Andrew Jackson, three weeks after a peace treaty had been signed. It was a war of confusion that did not result in any military gain for either side. The only thing that had been confirmed was the revolutionary spirit to go to war, and that might have kept Great Britain from going to war again with the United States.

Feeling Good?

Eris was quincunx the USA Sun as the administration of James Monroe began, ushering in what was known as "The Era of Good Feeling." Monroe was the last of the commanders of the American Revolution to serve as President. Some of the discords that took place during his term were beneficial to the United States. The Central American and South American nations began rebellions against Spain and started to set up their own republics. Andrew Jackson commanded a military expedition into Florida, ostensibly to fight the Indians, but mainly to pressure Spain into selling the territory to the United States.

In 1819, Eris was trine the USA Saturn, and a financial panic brought tension to the "Era of Good Feeling." The worst discord of the Monroe Administration was over the issue of slavery and what the Federal government role was to be. The Missouri territory was applying for statehood in the Union. There were fierce debates in the Congress as to whether it should be considered a slave state, since it was North of the other slave states. The rumblings of civil war had their beginnings in these arguments. Fortunately, a crisis was averted by the intervention of Henry Clay, the Great Compromiser, who worked out the agreement that Missouri would be a slave state and Maine would enter the Union as a free state. For thirty years, there would be an uneasy balance, with slave and free states entering the Union at the same time. Henry Clay had not resolved the arguments over civil war, but had merely postponed them.

In December, 1823, President Monroe revealed the foreign policy doctrine that bears his name, just as Eris was in opposition to the USA Midheaven. The Monroe Doctrine marked American ascendancy in the hemisphere, declaring that all territorial encroachment by European powers would be met with force. By this time, Spain had given up on her American colonies. The main purpose of the doctrine was to prevent colonization by the Russians, who were starting to explore below Alaska.

In 1826, for the 50th anniversary of Independence (marked by the deaths of Jefferson and Adams on the same day), Eris was squaring the USA Vesta. Far from causing discord, it was a period of security in hearth and home. Vesta also rules spiritual paths, including retreats from the outer world. This was a period of religious revival, and saw the growth of communal sects, from the Shakers (who abstained from sex) to the Mormons (who were accused of having too much sex.) This transit also marked the birth of the great American composer, Stephen Foster, whose most famous work was the song, "The Old Folks At Home."

Jacksonian Democracy

In 1829, with the inauguration of Andrew Jackson, Eris formed a Grand Trine in Air with the USA Juno and the USA Part of Fortune and a sextile to the USA Chiron. For the first time, the United States had a President not born in either Virginia or Massachusetts. Jacksonian Democracy was seen as opening up power to the masses, and wresting control from an aristocratic elite. Yet, such a change in power seemed to invite mob rule. This was especially apparent at Jackson's inauguration, when a mob of well-wishers stormed the White House. Furniture was smashed, and carpets and drapes were cut up as souvenirs. The mob only vacated the building when it was announced that liquor was being served on the front lawn.

With the coming of Jackson there arose a system of misfortune that would plague the Federal government for more than 50 years. The Jackson administration established the concept of "the Spoils System." ("To the Victor Belongs the Spoils.") Government jobs were to be held by political cronies and not by qualified persons. Until the coming of the Civil Service Act, each administration would see a transfer of government jobs, right down to the local post office. Each President would be besieged by herds of office seekers. It was a sinecure economy that provided wealth to political hacks.

Eris trine USA Juno was especially appropriate at the beginning of Jackson's administration, because there was a marital scandal which ended up bringing down Jackson's first cabinet. Secretary of War John Eaton had married Peggy O'Neale Timberlake, the daughter of a Washington tavern owner and the widow of sailor who had died at sea. Floride Calhoun, wife of Vice-President John C. Calhoun, and other society leaders did not think Peggy Eaton was of the right social class to be accepted by Washington society. Her reputation was smeared by stories claiming that she had an affair with Eaton before her sailor husband died. President Jackson called a cabinet meeting to denounce these stories, and it was the only cabinet meeting ever held to defend a woman's virtue. The social rancor grew so great that the cabinet ended up resigning in 1831. John and Peggy Eaton were sent off to represent the USA in the court of Spain.

In 1830, Eris was trine the USA Mars, and it marked an event that nearly resulted in civil war. In 1828, a very high tariff, known as "The Tariff of Abominations" was passed to protect the growing industries of the New England states. The Southern states, particularly South Carolina, felt the burden of this tariff, and they threatened secession over the issue. Vice-President Calhoun said that any state had the right to "nullify" a Federal law that was harmful to it. The climax of the debate took place at the Jefferson Day dinner on April 13, 1830, when President Jackson offered the toast, "The Union! It must be preserved!" Jackson threatened to raise an army against any state that dared to secede from the Union. South Carolina backed down on the issue, and a compromise was reached to reduce "The Tariff of Abominations."

This period also marked the beginning of the "Trail of Tears", the forcible relocation of Native Americans to West of the Mississippi. The state of Georgia wanted to seize land owned by the Cherokee, and Jackson used the U.S. Army to move the tribe to what is now Oklahoma. The Supreme Court ruled against Georgia's land grab, but Jackson refused to enforce the decision. Apart from a few missionaries, not many citizens were willing to speak up on behalf of the "savages." Ironically, the Cherokee were the most assimilated of the Native American tribes, having converted to Christianity, intermarried with white settlers, built houses and cabins, and even published their own newspaper. All of this did not matter to the U.S. Army which forced the tribe westward.

Although Jackson was victorious on the Nullification issue and Cherokee relocation, he had plenty of opposition to his policies. In the winter of 1833-1834, just as Eris was quincunx the USA Neptune, the Whig party was formed to oppose the policies of "King Andrew." The Whigs were a political chimera, made up by factions of old-time Federalists like Daniel Webster, states-rights advocates like Calhoun, and opportunists like Henry Clay. The only thing uniting them was a hatred of Jackson's politics. Once Jackson passed from the scene, the party started to break apart because of sectional differences, and it was not the sort of well-organized political machine like the Jacksonian Democrats.

In 1836, with Eris quincunx the USA Mercury, Americans were pleased to learn about a new republic on the continent. The ideas of freedom were being spread to the Republic of Texas. The defenders of the Alamo, particularly former Congressman Davy Crockett, were eulogized as martyrs for freedom. Former Tennessee Governor Sam Houston seemed like a new George Washington when he defeated General Antonio Lopez de Santa Anna (The Napoleon of the West) at the Battle of San Jacinto. With the United States approaching its 60th anniversary, the stories coming out of Texas helped carry the message of liberty and self-government.

However, on July 11, 1836, when Eris was conjunct the USA Moon, the Federal government issued the infamous Specie Circular, which would wreck the confidence of the American economy. The Specie Circular required that only gold or silver currency could be accepted for purchases of Federal lands. This created a drain on gold reserves which many banks could not support. By May, 1837, when Eris was conjunct the USA Pallas, most banks did not have the gold reserves to carry on business. Hundreds of banks failed around the country, creating a depression that lasted seven years. Pallas is the asteroid which rules development and social awareness, and those elements were cast into disarray during this aspect with Eris. The economic crisis was so bad that eight states ended up defaulting on bonds, causing major losses to foreign investors.

Chapter 11
Old Hickory Democracy

Eris in Capricorn

Andrew Jackson was born on March 15, 1767, three weeks after the death of his father. There was some question as to whether his birth was in North Carolina or South Carolina because he was born in the border town of Waxhaw. (Since the ACS Atlas puts Waxhaw in North Carolina, I have gone with that choice.) At his birth, Eris had just entered Capricorn, marking confusion and turmoil in areas of power and finance. Perhaps because of his impoverished youth, Jackson would be in conflict with people in power and financial leaders for most of his life. Banking institutions in particular would receive his greatest enmity.

In his early years, Jackson, his brothers, and his mother would live with relatives, mainly to perform acts of drudgery. They would never have a home they could call their own, and they were always branded as the "poor relations." As a child, with Eris trining his Neptune, Jackson was taken to the Presbyterian church for instruction. Eris squaring his Mercury showed a quick intellect, and Jackson was able to memorize the Presbyterian catechism at an early age.

Andrew Jackson
March 15, 1767
7:36 am LMT
Waxhaw, NC
Koch 34N55'28"
80W44'37"

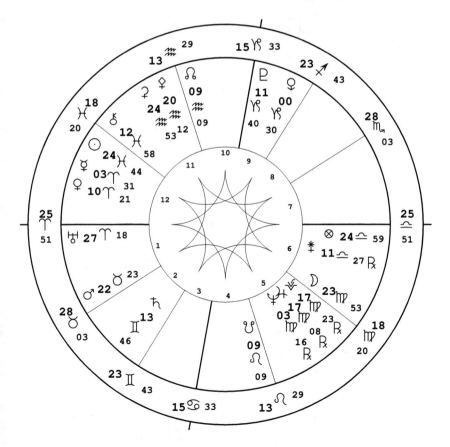

Jackson would grow up as the American Revolution took place, and the fighting would eventually get to his isolated area. At age 13, when Eris was square his Venus, he became a courier for a local regiment. His eldest brother, Hugh, died from heat stroke during the battle of Stono Ferry. As Eris was conjunct Jackson's Pluto and square his Juno, he witnessed one of the worst horrors of the war. Jackson was present in Waxhaw when the infamous Colonel Banastre Tarleton massacred more than 100 American soldiers who had attempted to surrender. Jackson later claimed that he was so close to Tarleton, he could have killed him.

All boys who were old enough to carry a musket were considered to be a threat to the British. In 1781, with Eris sextile his Chiron, Jackson and his brother, Robert, were taken prisoner. When Jackson refused to polish the boots of a British officer, he was slashed across the hand by the officer's sword. Robert was smashed on the head by the officer's sword when he refused to polish the boots. The brothers were taken to a prisoner of war camp where they contracted smallpox. Mrs. Jackson, who had been working as a nurse during the war, was able to gain their release. Robert died from smallpox and an infection to his wounded head. Mrs. Jackson nursed Andrew back to health and then went off to nurse sick nephews in Charleston. She would die from cholera in the autumn of 1781 and be buried in an unmarked grave.

When the Revolution ended, Eris was quincunx Jackson's Saturn, and he had lost his immediate family. He quarreled with his other relatives, who wanted nothing more to do with him. At this time, he came into a small inheritance, and visited Charleston. For the first time, he had contact with good society, and was introduced to the luxuries of fine clothing and gambling. When he returned to Waxhaw, he attempted saddle making and school teaching, neither of which went well as Eris passed over his Midheaven.

By 1785, with Eris trine his Jupiter and Vesta, Jackson moved to Salisbury, North Carolina, where he taught school, studied law, and developed a reputation as a rake. His most infamous act was to invite the town prostitutes to attend a society Christmas ball. Years later, an elderly Salisbury resident would declare, "If Andrew Jackson can become President, anybody can."[1] Jackson would be admitted to the bar in 1787, and in 1788 he would move to Nashville, Tennessee.

When Eris was trine Jackson's Mars in 1792, he was deeply involved in a relationship that would become a major source of contention in his life. When he moved to Nashville, he met and fell in love with Rachel Donelson Robards, a beautiful woman trapped in an unhappy marriage. Lewis Robards deserted his wife in 1790, and reports came that he had gotten a divorce in Virginia. Jackson married Rachel in 1791, only to discover two years later, when Eris was trine Jackson's Moon, that the divorce from Robards did not become effective until September, 1793. The couple was remarried in January 1794, when Eris was sextile Jackson's Sun. Though the Jacksons were happy together, for the rest of his life Jackson would fly into a murderous rage if anyone accused his wife of impropriety. Duels were fought over Mrs. Jackson's honor, and the matter of the marriage would play a major role in the course of Jackson's political career.

By 1795, with Eris squaring Jackson's Ascendant and Part of Fortune, he took a leading role in Tennessee politics. He became a delegate to the Tennessee constitutional convention, and when the state joined the Union, Jackson became a congressman. In 1797, with Eris squaring his Uranus, Jackson was chosen for the U.S. Senate, but he only served for one year. He became a judge on the Tennessee Supreme Court and served until 1804.

Eris in Aquarius

Eris was sextile Jackson's Mercury and quincunx his Neptune at a time when he started buying up property, which became his estate, the Hermitage. In 1803, he was involved in a street shoot-out with Governor John Sevier, who had dared to make a disparaging comment about Rachel Jackson. No one was killed in the shooting, though a stray bullet grazed one uninvolved man. For Jackson, to profane the name of Rachel was an unpardonable sin, like sinning against the Holy Ghost. In 1806, he would kill a man named Charles Dickinson, after receiving a bullet in the chest in a duel over Rachel.

During the War of 1812, Eris was conjunct Jackson's North

Node and opposing his South Node. It was during this conflict that he achieved a reputation as America's leading warrior, and got the nickname of "Old Hickory" because of his toughness. Jackson commanded the Tennessee militia, and organized a campaign against the Creek Indians in Georgia and Alabama. The Creek War ended in 1814, when Eris was sextile Jackson's Venus, and the Creek Indians were forced to give up 20 million acres of land for white settlement. It was the start of Jackson's reputation as a rapacious enemy of Native Americans. However, at the time, Jackson adopted an orphaned Creek baby, and intended that the child should go to West Point, but he died from an illness in 1828 before that plan was realized.

In 1815, with Eris trine Jackson's Juno, he won the greatest victory of the war at the Battle of New Orleans. The war had been over for three weeks when the battle took place. Yet, Jackson's fame would be enshrined by the military success. Three hundred British soldiers were killed and 1200 were wounded as they marched against American lines fortified with heavy bales of cotton. Only 13 American soldiers died in the battle. After the stalemate of war in the North, and the disheartening burning of Washington, DC, Jackson's victory captured the public imagination. The downside to this fame was that it put a strain on Jackson's marriage, since Rachel was a simple woman who did not enjoy lavish public events. When Jackson received songs of praise in his honor and was crowned with a laurel wreath, Rachel wrote, "I wept when I saw this idolatry."[2]

Jackson's Florida campaign of 1818 took place when Eris was entering his Eleventh House and trine his Saturn. It was a military attack against Indians in Florida, and its purpose was to pressure the Spanish into selling Florida to the United States. An international controversy was started when two Englishmen were found among the Indians. Jackson declared the two men to be British spies, who were stirring up the Indians against the Americans. The Englishmen were hanged, provoking major protests from the British government. Secretary of War, John C. Calhoun (who later became Jackson's Vice-President) denounced the hangings in a cabinet meeting and insisted Jackson should be removed from command. The Secretary of State, John Quincy Adams, defended Jackson's military campaign and President Monroe decided to leave Jackson in command.

By 1824, any amiability between John Quincy Adams and Andrew Jackson had vanished with the dirty politics of the Presidential election. Eris was quincunx Jackson's Jupiter and Vesta. Although he won the popular vote, he did not get enough of a majority to win the electoral vote. The election had to be decided by the House of Representatives. John Quincy Adams supposedly cut a deal with opposing candidate Henry Clay. In the House, Clay used his influence to sway Congressmen to vote for Adams, and Clay became Secretary of State in the Adams administration. Jackson would denounce Clay as "the Judas of the West". For the next four years, Jackson would spread the word that the will of the people had been thwarted, and he promoted the idea that only he was the true man of the people.

It was also at this time that Jackson blessed the wedding of Andrew and Emily Donelson, who became his family and heirs. Andrew and Emily were both Rachel's relatives. Jackson saw Andrew as a political protégé. Emily Donelson would become Jackson's White House hostess, when tragic events brought about the death of Rachel Jackson in 1828. The supporters of John Quincy Adams had used the embarrassing story of the Jackson marriage as a campaign talking point. Jackson managed to shield his wife from the humiliation. Yet, after the election, Rachel accidentally overheard an editor speaking about the smears against her character. The shock of it broke her spirit, and she died shortly after from heart failure. Jackson said he would never forgive his political enemies for what they had done to his wife, and that attitude would bring about a political crisis in his new administration.

Andrew Jackson became Seventh President of the United States while Eris was conjunct his Pallas, and he would unwisely be embroiled in a social conflict that would lead to political trouble. Secretary of War John Eaton had married an attractive widow, Peggy O'Neale Timberlake. Floride Calhoun and wives of the cabinet members did not approve of Peggy's Eaton social pedigree.

They socially ostracized her and spread rumors that Peggy and John had conducted an adulterous affair before their marriage.

For Jackson, this was like the attacks on Rachel all over again. Defending Peggy Eaton became the standard of loyalty to Jackson. Even Emily Donelson was banished from the White House for a while because she would not support Peggy. While Southern Democrats like Calhoun disparaged Peggy, Northern Democrats like Secretary of State Martin Van Buren supported her in society. The result was that much patronage in the Jackson administration went to the Northern Democrats.

The issue was finally defused in 1831, when Jackson's cabinet resigned, but Jackson never forgot Van Buren's loyalty nor Calhoun's treachery. From that time forward, Van Buren's political fortunes would rise, and Calhoun's career would decline. (In the 1860's, historian James Parton would write a great Freudian slip with the line, "The political history of the United States, for the last thirty years, dates from the moment when the soft hand of Mr. Van Buren touched Mrs. Eaton's knocker.")[3]

In 1832, with Eris square Jackson's Mars, he was victorious in two major conflicts. First was the Black Hawk War, a Native American uprising near Illinois, which was crushed by a thousand Federal troops. Second was the veto of the charter of the Bank of the United States, the national bank that handled government finances. To Jackson, the bank symbolized an aristocratic money monopoly, which could influence the policies of government. Henry Clay had forced the charter passage through Congress to make it a campaign issue in 1832. The voters sided with Jackson and saw the Bank of the United States as a corrupt institution that should not be trusted with deposits of the government's funds.

Eris was conjunct Jackson's Ceres in 1836, as he was making plans for his retirement. His hopes for a happy return to the Hermitage were dashed by the news that Emily Donelson was afflicted with tuberculosis. It was a lingering and painful illness through the summer and autumn, and Emily finally died on Dec. 16, 1836. Jackson would leave office with Eris sextile his Ascendant and trine his Part of Fortune, still retaining his popularity, despite the abuse the Whig party threw at him. In fact, the Whigs would depict the retired Jackson as the main power behind the scenes of the Van Buren administration, running things as if he never left the Presidency.

In 1838, with Eris sextile his Uranus, Jackson still remained very popular, but the administration of Martin Van Buren had to deal with the misfortunes of a financial panic, which some said was the result of Jackson's policies. Whenever he traveled, admirers would mob Jackson. He continued to express opinions and guide the course of the Democratic Party on major issues, such as statehood for Texas. Jackson died on June 8, 1845, just as Eris was sextile his natal Eris. According to legend, a visitor approached a slave at the Hermitage and asked him if he thought Jackson had gone to Heaven. The slave's response was, "If General Jackson wants to go, who's going to stop him?" [4]

Endnotes:

[1] Meacham, Jon, *American Lion: Andrew Jackson in the White House,* Random House Trade Paperback, New York, 2009, 978-0-8129-7346-4, page 20.

[2] Ibid, page 33
[3] Ibid, page 74
[4] Ibid, page 346

Chapter 12
The Cock of Kentucky

Natal Discord

With Eris squaring his Mercury, Henry Clay had a brilliant talent as an orator, becoming known as one of the greatest speakers in the history of the United States. Eris quincunx Uranus allowed him to appear as wild and dramatic as a revolutionary, even when he was supporting reactionary causes. Like a rooster announcing the dawn, Clay would strut and crow in his political posturing, sometimes to the detriment of the country, but always for the benefit of Henry Clay. Author Irving Stone would describe his rhetorical abilities:

> "He was always more interested in how he said a thing than in what he had to say; more interested in the emotional effect he had upon his listeners, his ability to bend them to his will, to achieve his desired ends than in the nature of the material he was presenting, its validity or usefulness. As a result his mind became a swift-flowing, shallow mountain torrent." [1]

Eris in Capricorn

Henry Clay would sometimes tell people that he had been raised as an orphan boy in an environment of poverty and ignorance. In truth,

Henry Clay
April 12, 1777
12:00 LMT
Hanover, VA
Koch 37N15'59"
77W22'14"

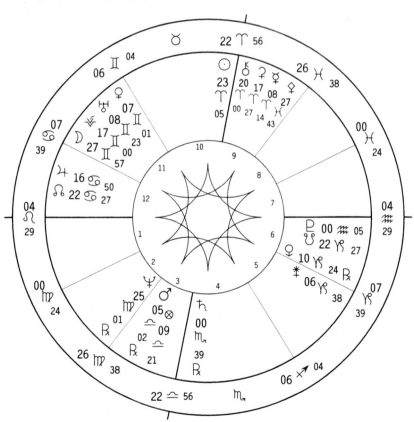

he came from a very large and well off family. His mother gave birth to twenty children (nine by Henry's father, and eleven by her second husband.) Unfortunately, Mrs. Clay did not write down Henry's birth time, and we have to use Noon for the chart, which prevents any discussion of house cusps and Moon positions. Henry's father owned a 460-acre farm that had eighteen slaves working it. When Mr. Clay died in 1781, young Henry was given two slaves as part of his inheritance.

In the 1780's, when transiting Eris was opposing Henry's Jupiter, squaring his Ceres, and quincunx his Vesta, Mrs. Clay married Captain Henry Watkins, who proved to be a very kind stepfather. Watkins moved the family to Richmond, and got young Henry a job as a clerk in a store. In 1788, with Eris square his Chiron, Henry attended meetings of the Virginia legislature, and listened to Patrick Henry, James Monroe, and James Madison debate whether Virginia should ratify the new Constitution. These debates had a profound effect on Henry and inspired him to become an orator.

In 1792, with Eris conjunct Henry's South Node and opposing his North Node, Captain Watkins moved his family to Kentucky, but he allowed Henry to remain in Richmond. Through his influence, Watkins got Henry a position as a clerk in the Court of Chancery. It was there he developed an interest in the law, and he met George Wythe, who had trained Thomas Jefferson in the law.

With Eris squaring Henry's Sun, George Wythe became Henry's benefactor, training him in legal procedure. Wythe tried to interest Henry in books and literature, but he did not learn much from reading. Henry Clay preferred oral lessons, always recalling what was said to him. When Eris was trine his Neptune, he spent his days listening to court cases, and studying the presentations of the lawyers. He spent his evenings at the Richmond Debating Club, listening to the speakers and developing his own voice.

At age 21, with Eris sextile Pallas, Henry Clay was admitted to the bar. He then moved to Kentucky where he developed a thriving legal practice. He married Lucretia Hart, who was a member of a prominent Kentucky family. They had eleven children, but only four of them outlived Henry Clay. Lucretia Clay outlived her husband by twelve years.

Eris in Aquarius

Henry Clay leaped into Kentucky politics with impetuous haste. By the time Eris moved into Aquarius and was conjunct his Pluto and square his Saturn, he was on his way to practicing what George Orwell would later call "Doublespeak", which was the ability to hold two contradictory opinions simultaneously. Irving Stone would describe this two-faced attitude:

"He had become known as the defender of the poor, the downtrodden, and the unfortunate, and so he was when he could make a great show of it in a public courtroom; but on the business side of his practice he served the money interests. He fought for the right of owners to employ women and children in the early factories on the sophistry that, 'Constant occupation is the best security for innocence and virtue, and idleness is the parent of vice and crime.' He opposed all control of labor exploitation on the grounds that exploitation arose out of the nature of man, and was inescapable." [2]

Henry Clay would start his political career by advocating the gradual release of slaves. Within a few years, he would be busy purchasing slaves. He became an advocate for Fugitive Slave Laws, and promoted the introduction of slavery into the new states added to the Union.

In 1806, when transiting Eris was trine his Mars, Henry Clay took on his most high-profile law case by defending former Vice-President Aaron Burr against charges of treason. Clay managed to get Burr released with a verdict of "Not Proven." Years later, Clay was shocked when he received reports, particularly one from Thomas Jefferson, which convinced him that Burr had been part of a conspiracy. The next time Clay encountered Burr, he refused to shake his hand.

With Eris trine Venus in 1811, Clay was elected to the U.S. House of Representatives, and was chosen as Speaker of the House on his first day, the only time in U.S. History that ever happened. As Speaker, he maneuvered committee appointments for his cronies, who formed a faction known as the War Hawks. They were advocating war with Great Britain in order to annex Canada. By 1812, with Eris trine his Uranus and sextile Mercury, Henry Clay had the influence to get a declaration of war through the Congress with a majority of eight votes.

The War of 1812 went badly for the United States and Clay left the Congress and was sent to Europe to help negotiate an end to the war. With the help of John Quincy Adams and other diplomats, Clay was able to sign the Treaty of Ghent, which ended the war, providing no benefits to either Great Britain or the United States. Clay stayed in Europe for a few months to negotiate a commercial treaty with Great Britain.

Upon his return to America, Clay supported the charter for the Second Bank of the United States. He became a founding member of the American Colonization Society, which intended to send freed slaves to Liberia. Clay became furious that President James Monroe had appointed John Quincy Adams as Secretary of State instead of himself. During the Monroe administration, Clay used his influence in Congress to obstruct and hinder all work by Monroe and Adams. The only constructive effort by Clay during this period was to broker the Compromise of 1820 and delay a break-up of the Union.

By 1824, with Eris quincunx his Jupiter, Clay was determined to run for President, even though there were three other major candidates in the field. Clay finished fourth, but no candidate had a majority of electoral votes, and the election had to be decided by the House of Representatives. Clay offered his support to John Quincy Adams, allegedly in return for being appointed Secretary of State.

One story of the House vote on the election tells of a New York congressman who could not decide on which candidate to vote for. When it came time for him to vote, the congressman fell to his knees in prayer, asking for divine guidance in his vote. A paper fluttered to the floor in front of him, and on the paper was the name of John Quincy Adams. The devout congressman immediately took this as a sign and cast his vote for Adams. Only later would it be noted that the handwriting on the paper belonged to Henry Clay.

With Eris trine his Vesta and sextile his Ceres, Clay became Secretary of State. He found it to be a dull job, because he could not use his skills as an orator. He devoted himself to his duties in the hope that he would succeed Adams as President. However, political forces were working against Adams and Clay, as Andrew Jackson (the winner of the popular vote in 1824) denounced the infamous bargain that had thwarted the will of the people. By 1828, the public tide had turned, and Adams and Clay found themselves cast out of the political scene by the tidal wave of Jacksonian Democracy.

For two years, with Eris sextile his Chiron, Clay remained at his estate, Ashland, and brooded over his political fortune. In 1831, the Kentucky legislature sent him to the U.S. Senate, where he became the leading political figure opposing Andrew Jackson. With Eris quincunx his North Node, but also sextile his Sun, he entered the Presidential campaign of 1832 opposing Jackson. Clay tried to create a political issue out of Jackson's veto for the charter of the Bank of the United States. Unfortunately for Clay, he did not realize how unpopular the institution was with the public, and Jackson won support for his veto.

With Eris quincunx his Neptune, Clay began organizing the formation of the Whig Party. He managed to bring in all manner of disaffected political factions; Anti-Masons, Anti-Catholics, Anti-Labor, Anti-Free Trade, and the perennial State Rights advocates. Behind the scenes, he helped defuse the Nullification crisis by lowering the tariff that had enraged South Carolina. He expected to be the Whig nominee in 1836 but was disappointed when the Whigs chose General William Henry Harrison, who ended up losing to Martin Van Buren.

Harrison would be re-nominated in 1840, much to the fury of Clay who declared, "My friends are not worth the powder and shot it would take to kill them."[3] To mollify Clay, the Whigs offered him the Vice-Presidency, which he refused. Ironically, Clay passed up his best chance to become President, since Harrison died from pneumonia after a month as President, and John Tyler became the first Vice-President to succeed to the Presidency.

Clay acted as a gadfly to the Tyler administration, working

behind the scenes to foil any legislative activity. In 1844, Clay set himself up as the leading Whig candidate to be nominated for President. The Democratic Party ended up nominating James Polk, who was considered to be a non-entity. The Whigs asked the taunting question, "Who is James Polk?" The public quickly learned there was nothing negative to say about Polk, whereas there was plenty to complain about Clay in his long career. Clay was denounced for gambling, dueling, drinking, and making shady political deals. In the end, Clay would lose his third run for the Presidency by 37,000 votes.

Eris in Pisces

When Eris moved into Pisces, it trined Clay's Saturn, and he was relegated to the role of elder statesman. He still had admirers, including an upcoming Whig Congressman named Abraham Lincoln, who visited Clay at Ashland. After losing the chance for the Whig nomination in 1848, Clay left the Senate for a year, but was sent back again in 1849, just as new controversies were brewing between North and South. Once again, Clay was prevailed upon to exercise his influence as "the Great Compromiser."

Unfortunately, the Compromise of 1850 helped undo the benefits of the Compromise of 1820. California was admitted to the Union as a free state, in exchange for a Federal Fugitive Slave Law. Clay proved to be the devil that got Daniel Webster, by getting the New England statesman to support the Fugitive Slave Law. This so shocked Webster's supporters that they considered him to be a lost soul, forever damned by supporting slavery.

Clay continued to serve until his death on June 29, 1852 from tuberculosis. He was the first person to lie in state in the U.S. Capitol. In 1957, when Eris was sextile Clay's Uranus and approaching a square to Clay's natal Eris, Senator John F. Kennedy chaired a committee that named Henry Clay as one of the five greatest Senators in U.S. History. Still, his reputation remains murky because of his political intrigue. Perhaps Irving Stone offers the best final commentary:

"Henry Clay said, 'I would rather be right than be President.' This was the sourest grape since Aesop originated the fable." [4]

Endnotes:

[1] Stone, Irving, *They Also Ran*, Pyramid Books, New York, 1964, pages 46-47

[2] Ibid, page 48

[3] Ibid, page 60

[4] Ibid, page 43

Chapter 13

Old Abe Lincoln
Came Out of the Wilderness

Eris in Aquarius

Abraham Lincoln was born with Eris sextile his Neptune, Saturn, Midheaven, Vesta and Venus, and squaring his Nodes. His historical image would be subjected to a variety of interpretations. For lofty issues, he would be remembered as "Father Abraham", a mystical figure guided by prophetic dreams and a divine mandate to end slavery. For mundane matters, he would be remembered as a crafty politician with a shrewish wife, never destined to find any peace of mind. The real Abraham Lincoln may be found somewhere between these two extremes.

Abraham Lincoln was born and raised in backwoods Kentucky. Eris was in the Twelfth House, and the Lincoln family was fairly isolated for several years. They struggled with farm life in Kentucky until 1816, when a lawsuit over property forced them to leave the farm. Thomas Lincoln, Abraham's father, never approved of slavery, and would not use slave labor on his farm. As a result, his farm was never as prosperous as those that had slaves.

Abraham Lincoln
February 12, 1809
6:54 am LMT
Hodgenville, KY
Koch 37N34'26"
85W44'24"

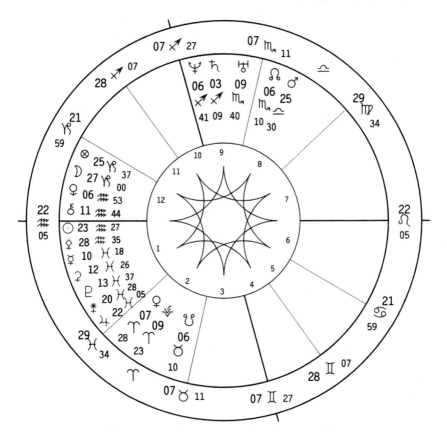

With Eris conjunct Lincoln's Chiron, the family moved to Indiana, where Abraham's mother died from "Milk sickness", caused by drinking the milk of an animal that ate White Snakeroot. Thomas Lincoln was quickly remarried to a woman named Sarah Bush Johnston, who developed a close bond to her stepson, Abraham. Through her influence, Lincoln would continue with book learning, although he only had 18 months of formal schooling.

The Lincoln family moved to Illinois in 1830, and the following year young Abraham set out on his own. By the time Eris was conjunct Lincoln's Ascendant and Sun in 1835, he had settled in the town of New Salem, and made a name for himself as a shopkeeper, a postmaster, and a very good wrestler. He met the first love of his life Ann Rutledge and they pledged to be married. Ann died in August, 1835, and the loss sent Lincoln into a deep depression, a malady that effected him many times in his life.

Lincoln would not be married until November, 1842, when he finally agreed, after much hesitation to marry Mary Todd from Kentucky. It was a marriage that produced four sons and a clash of temperaments. Some Lincoln biographers, including his old law partner William Herndon, have suggested that Lincoln's deep involvement in politics was a way to get away from his nagging wife.

Eris in Pisces

As Eris was conjunct Lincoln's Pallas in the mid-1840's, he became more involved in Whig politics and made political connections in the Illinois legislature. In 1846, he became a Whig Congressman, noted for questioning the honesty of President Polk regarding the start of the Mexican War. By the time Eris in Pisces was squaring his Saturn, Lincoln was tired of national politics and settled in to a lucrative legal practice, establishing a reputation as a wise and clever court lawyer.

In the 1850's, with the rise of the Republican Party and the growing controversy over slavery, Lincoln was persuaded to again enter the political arena. In 1858, with Eris square his Neptune, Lincoln ran for the Senate against his old political rival, Stephen A. Douglas. The Lincoln-Douglas debates would bring national attention to Lincoln and his political views. Though he did not advocate abolition of slavery, he was against its spread to the territories. Douglas won the election to the Senate, but Lincoln won a moral victory and became the Republican candidate for President in 1860.

When Lincoln took office, Southern states seceded from the Union, and Lincoln had to call up volunteers to put down the rebellion. The fighting would last four bloody years, while Eris was trine Lincoln's Uranus. The war became exceedingly deadly because of changes in technology, with improved rifles, telegraph lines, balloons, and ironclad ships bringing faster military actions. Lincoln would support the development of these new weapons, and would support any general who showed innovation and determination in winning battles. In spite of military defeats and political dissension, Lincoln would manage to hold on to power against all odds, winning re-election in 1864.

The victory in April, 1865 would bring little comfort because the nation was plunged into grief over the shooting of Lincoln on April 14. As with the death of Alexander Hamilton, transiting Eris was trine Mars (in the Eighth House) at the time of the assassination. Eris was also sextile Pluto and squaring the Moon and the Ascendant. The killing had been part of a conspiracy to kill leaders of the government, but only Lincoln had been killed. The shooting would spark emotional and religious mourning throughout the world, except in die-hard parts of the former Confederacy. Yet, there were Southern leaders, such as Robert E. Lee, who expressed shock and horror over the assassination.

Lincoln would be designated as the final casualty of the Civil War, which was technically not correct since there were some skirmishes going on for a few weeks, but his death appeared as a poetic culmination of the national tragedy. Immediately he would become mythologized as a fallen martyr to the cause of freedom, and all faults and failings would be glossed over or forgotten. His Secretary of War Edwin Stanton would immortalize him with the words, "Now he belongs to the Ages!"

Yet, the death of Lincoln would not end the spirit of discord. In 1876, when Eris was conjunct Lincoln's Pluto, there was a plot by a gang of counterfeiters to steal the body of Lincoln

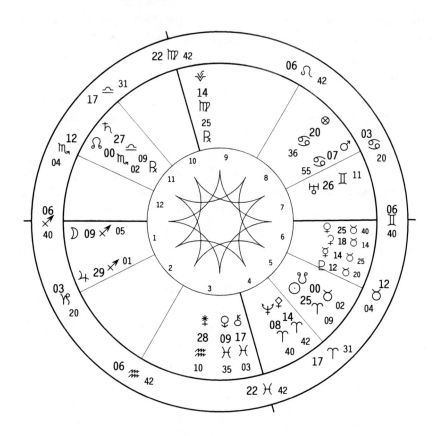

Lincoln Assassination
April 14, 1865, 10:00 pm LMT
Washington DC
Koch 38N53'42" 77W02'12"

from his tomb and hold it for ransom. Secret Service agents foiled the plot, chasing the culprits from the tomb and later rounding them up. The criminals were later released on the technicality that Illinois did not have a law against grave robbing. For years afterward, the body of Lincoln, as well as the body of Mary Todd Lincoln, received several reburials to discourage other grave robbers. Finally, in 1901, with Eris conjunct Lincoln's Jupiter, the body of Lincoln was placed in a new tomb, and buried under tons of concrete to prevent any further tampering.

Part III

Eris in Pisces

Fishy Business

Eris entered Pisces just in time for the Mexican War, but the planet did not make any transits to the USA chart until 1852. Eris was trine the USA Venus, and it marked an end to peacemaking between the North and the South. Henry Clay's attempt at a Compromise of 1850 had disrupted the balance of power between free and slave states. California was allowed to enter the Union as a free state, if a Fugitive Slave Law was passed. Northern states had previously circumvented Fugitive Slave Laws by passing anti-kidnapping laws, but this law superseded state law, giving Federal sanction to slavery.

Eris trine USA Venus was the period when the Whig party fractured, and the remnants would help form the nucleus of the Republican party. One political faction that acquired power at the time was the strongly nativist American party. This was a party devoted to the issues of Anti-Immigration and Anti-Catholicism. Its members did not have set opinions on the other issues of the day. When asked political questions, they would respond with the statement, "I don't know." As a result, they became branded as "The Know-Nothings", and after a few years their political strength would melt away.

The election of Franklin Pierce as President was supposed to provide a peaceful balance in the nation. Pierce chose a cabinet that was half Northern and half Southern. (To this day, he holds the record of being the only President serving a full term who did not have any cabinet member resign.) The spirit of peacemaking came to an end with the Kansas-Nebraska Act, which allowed the citizens of Kansas territory to decide whether they would allow slavery. "Bleeding Kansas" became a rehearsal for the Civil War in the next decade as bands of Abolitionist settlers waged war against bands of Pro-Slavery settlers.

As Eris trined the USA Jupiter, a recession was afflicting the nation. Then the Supreme Court announced the Dred Scott Decision, which declared "a black man has no rights which a white man is bound to respect." This sparked Abolitionist outrage across the country, especially over the prospect of extending slavery to the territories. With Eris quincunx the USA North Node, the revulsion over the extension of slavery became so great, a preacher named John Brown attempted to spark a slave rebellion by seizing the arsenal at Harper's Ferry in order to provide arms to slaves willing to fight for their freedom. Brown was beaten by Colonel Robert E. Lee, and hanged for treason, becoming a martyr for the Abolitionists.

The Civil War

With the election of Abraham Lincoln and the secession of the Southern states, the march to Civil War became inevitable. Eris made her bloodiest transits in 1863, by squaring the USA Uranus, trining the USA Ascendant, conjunct the USA Ceres, and sextile her own natal position. Uranus provided the technical skills for new weapons, and replaced the old battlefield tactics with innovative strategies, such as Sherman's March to the Sea. Eris trine the Ascendant gave conflicting images of both sides in the war. The Southerners saw the Yankees as invaders. The Northerners saw themselves as liberators for the enslaved population. Eris conjunct Ceres brought an end to any notion of slavery as a "nurturing" institution, and the agrarian South had its economy ruined.

With Eris sextile Eris there was so much military confusion that victory eventually went to the side that made the least mistakes. Generals who were promoted because of their political connections made major battlefield mistakes when fighting officers who had West Point educations. Both Abraham Lincoln and Jefferson Davis had to fight off dissension from within, and deal with politicians who thought they could do a better job managing the war.

Fort Sumter

When Abraham Lincoln was inaugurated, he was open to the idea of a negotiated settlement that would keep the South in the Union. While there was some talk of reconciliation, the Confederate states kept raising armies and urging other states to join their cause. One main item of contention was the location of Federal forts in Confederate territory, particularly Fort Sumter on an island in the middle of Charleston harbor. For months, there had been local negotiations with the Sumter troops, and then an effort to starve them out. When Lincoln announced that he was sending ships to provision the fort, the Confederate army took this as a signal to attack.

Artillery was set up around Charleston harbor, and at 4:30 am on April 12, 1861, the barrage began, officially starting the Civil War. In the chart for this event, Eris in the Twelfth House is sextile Pluto in the Second House, and squaring Mars and Uranus in the Third House. It would be the start of the extreme violence that would transform the nation over the next four years. Men would march off to war with visions of military glory, only to face the grim reality of mass killing on the battlefields.

Fort Sumter would surrender after more than 30 hours of bombardment. Ironically, the only Union dead would be two soldiers blasted by exploding cartridges while firing a cannon salute marking the surrender of the fort. News of the attack would galvanize both North and South, bringing more states into the Confederacy, and spurring Northerners to volunteer to preserve national honor.

Gettysburg

The high-water mark for the Confederacy would come at a small town in Pennsylvania, hitherto only known for its seminary and its shoe factory. It was the shoe factory that attracted Confederate soldiers who had invaded Pennsylvania, and they came to the town in the hopes of getting shoes for their army. Approaching the town from the North, they ran into the Union army coming from the South. The first Union soldier would shoot at the Confederates at 7:30 am, July 1, 1863, starting the battle of Gettysburg.

In the chart for the beginning of the battle, Eris is conjunct the Eighth House cusp and Chiron, marking an event that would see approximately 50,000 casualties and turn the small town into a national cemetery. Eris sextile Pallas formed a Yod (double quincunx) to Mars in Leo (conjunct the Ascendant), and Juno sextile Mars formed a Yod to Eris. The Yod aspect is also known as "the finger of God", or "the finger of destiny", or even "the flying fickle finger of fate." It is supposed to mark a person or event that has a special destiny.

If ever there was a battle that would please the goddess of discord and the god of war, Gettysburg was the textbook case. Over a three day period, the two armies would maul each other in

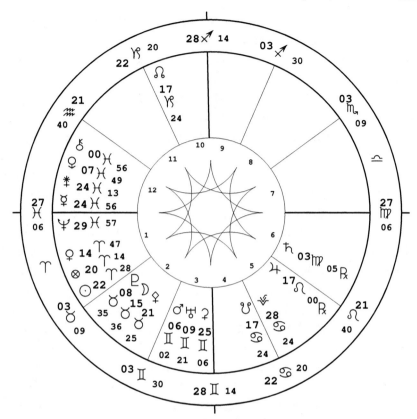

Battle of Fort Sumter
April 12, 1861, 4:30 am LMT
Charleston, SC
Koch 32N45'35" 79W55'52"

furious attacks, leaving thousands of dead soldiers strewn over the battlefield. The Confederate army sealed its fate on the first day by not securing the high ground, particularly a hill known as Little Round Top. Without the high ground, Confederate artillery could not hit the Union line on Cemetery Ridge, and the Union army would block further advancement into Pennsylvania.

With Eris sextile Pallas and trine the Sun, conventional military wisdom was turned on its head. Union Colonel Joshua Lawrence Chamberlain, ordered to hold Little Round Top, managed to beat back the Confederate attack, not by sitting still as expected, but by leading a charge with a flanking maneuver. This caused the

Confederate attackers to surrender. On the final day of the battle, General Robert E. Lee gambled everything on a charge by General George Pickett's division against the fortified Union line. Even though a similar charge, ordered by Union general Ambrose Burnside, had failed horribly at the battle of Fredericksburg, Lee attempted the same sort of charge at Gettysburg with the same horrible results. (The Confederacy was definitely in trouble when its greatest general was using the tactics of the Union's worst general.)

With Eris quincunx Juno, both North and South would be united by the horror of the ferocity of the battle and the casualties. Abraham Lincoln would later speak of the "honored dead" giving "the last full measure of their devotion", and it would be true of both sides in the battle. With Eris square the North and South Nodes of the battle, Gettysburg would be remembered as hallowed ground for North and South.

On July 4, 1863, Lee and the Confederate army began their retreat from Pennsylvania. At the same time, word came of General Ulysses S. Grant's victory at Vicksburg, which split the Confederacy. From that time on, it would become a defensive war for the South. With Grant taking command in Virginia and William Tecumseh Sherman marching through Georgia, the Confederacy would be further divided and experience terrible devastation. Peace would come with Lee's surrender at Appomattox Court House on April 9, 1865, and the nation would begin an uneasy period of Reconstruction.

From Sacrifice to Avarice

After the carnage of the Civil War, the next Eris contact with the USA chart was a trine to the USA Sun in 1874. The country was in an economic depression caused by a financial panic the previous year. Stories were coming out about widespread corruption caused by politicians. The news of the Tweed Ring, the Whiskey Ring, and the Credit Mobilier scandals showed how much corporations were buying off political leaders, and how politicians were providing favors for corporations. The public image of the United States was that of a greedy oligarchy, with fortunes being made by the social elite to the detriment of the general population. It was

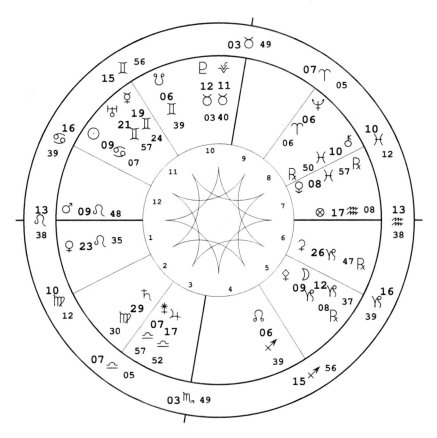

Battle of Gettysburg
July 1, 1863
7:30 am LMT
Koch 39N49'51" 77 W13'53"

a time of nouveau riche gaudiness, which Mark Twain would satirize as "The Gilded Age."

By the time of America's Centennial in 1876, as Eris was nearing the USA Fifth house and quincunx the USA Saturn, the focus turned to scientific creativity, hard-work, and rising industry. At the Philadelphia Exposition, new inventions such as Alexander Graham Bell's new telephone became featured attractions. Thomas Edison was just setting up his laboratory in Menlo Park, NJ and he invented the first mimeograph machine, the phonograph, and started work on the electric light. Businesses were finding ways to exploit new machinery, though new developments would displace old-time workers. Andrew Carnegie built the first modern steel mill, which would revolutionize the steel industry, and take away work from the old forges. It was a time when the craftsman was being replaced by the machine operator.

In 1884, Eris was quincunx the USA Midheaven, at a time when Grover Cleveland was elected President, ending a quarter century of Republican rule and bringing in a reform administration that would champion Civil Service changes. The 1884 election was messy, with Republican candidate James G. Blaine being charged with corrupt political practices, and Democratic candidate Cleveland being charged with impropriety in his private life. Voters decided a good public figure was more important than private life issues. So, they elected Cleveland because his public life was blameless, and they returned Blaine to his private life which was blameless.

Wounded Knee

For the previous century, the U.S. government had been practising a doctrine of "exceptionalism" in regard to the Native Americans. "Exceptionalism" promotes the idea that a nation is "exceptional" and normal rules of conduct and morality do not reply. This allowed the Federal government to send in troops to take the land of Native Americans, to massacre the buffalo in order to deprive tribes of a food supply, and to break all treaties negotiated with various chiefs. Native American tribes were confined to reservations and allowed rations, courtesy of the Great White Father in Washington D.C.

In the 1880's, a millennialist movement rose up amongst the Native Americans. Medicine Men began advocating the Ghost Dance, which was a frenetic circular dance that was intended to summon back dead ancestors and establish a new world full of nature's bounty. What made the Indian agents nervous was that this new world was supposed to be devoid of white men. Some in the military regarded the Ghost Dance as signaling a new uprising by the tribes.

In December, 1890, troops were sent into South Dakota to suppress the Ghost Dance cult. The prominent chief, Sitting

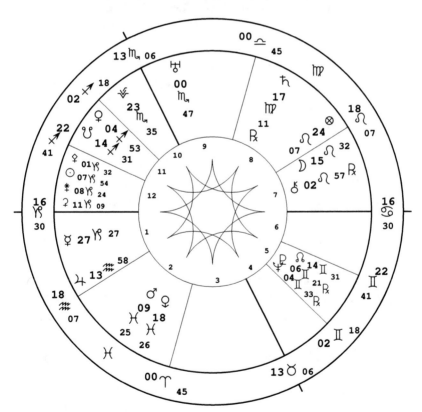

Wounded Knee
December 29, 1890
8:00 am MST
Koch 43N08'26" 102 W21'55"

Bull, was killed by Native American police officers, supposedly for resisting arrest. The followers of Sitting Bull fled to the camp of his brother, Spotted Elk. On December 28, 1890, the camp of Spotted Elk was surrounded by the Seventh Cavalry. On the morning of December 29, Colonel James Forsyth ordered the surrender of all weapons, and demanded that the tribe be removed from the area. Many were willing to comply with the demands, but there were a minority of Ghost Dancers who wanted to resist.

The men of the tribe began to gather at 8 am, when Eris was sextile the Ascendant. A Medicine Man named Yellow Bird jumped up and started performing the Ghost Dance. A deaf warrior named Black Coyote refused to surrender his rifle, possibly because he did not hear the order. Five warriors were accused of pointing their guns at the troopers. At that point, the surrounding soldiers opened fire on the crowd, killing the warriors, as well as Spotted Elk and numerous women and children. The shooting continued into the afternoon, and many of the wounded were left to freeze to death when a blizzard covered the area. Casualty estimates put the Native American dead at more than 150.

Eris opposing Saturn and quincunx the Moon would mark the final massacre of the Indian wars. Eris was squaring the North and South Nodes, and there would be reconsideration of the policies toward Native Americans. General Nelson Miles blamed Colonel Forsyth for the massacre and relieved him of command, but Forsyth was cleared by an Army Court of Inquiry and reinstated. Nevertheless, General Miles would continue to speak against Forsyth and tried in vain to keep him from getting promotions.

At the time, news of the Wounded Knee massacre was greeted with praise in the rest of the nation. L. Frank Baum, the future creator of the land of Oz, wrote a chilling editorial suggesting the extermination of all Native Americans lest they cause trouble for future generations. Fortunately, others were not so inclined towards genocide. Native Americans would finally be given United States citizenship in 1924.

A moving moment took place when the bodies of the Wounded Knee victims were placed in a mass grave three days after the massacre. General Leonard Colby heard some faint crying, and he uncovered a baby girl who had survived the massacre and the following blizzard. Colby adopted the baby girl, Little Lost Bird. Unfortunately, he also exploited her and she appeared at sideshows as the last survivor of Wounded Knee. Little Lost Bird would die at age 30, rejected by both the white and Native American cultures.

Ironically, the phrase "Bury my heart at Wounded Knee" was written as a joke. In 1931, the poet Stephen Vincent Benet wrote a poem on unusual "American Names." Not knowing of the massacre, he thought it would be amusing if his heart were buried at a place called Wounded Knee. In 1970, historian Dee Brown would use the phrase for his best-selling book *Bury My Heart At Wounded Knee*, which would raise public awareness of the massacre.

America Strikes Out

The next Eris contact with the USA chart would not be until 1893, when Eris was sextile the USA Vesta. A serious depression shut down American industry. There was five times as much paper money in circulation than there was gold in the treasury. Bond issues to bring in more gold were a failure, and there was mass unemployment when businesses failed. More demands were made for the Federal government to help the unemployed.

In 1894, when Eris was squaring the U.S. Part of Fortune and quincunx the USA Juno, a mass movement arose to protest the lack of help from the Federal government. Jacob Coxey began a march from Ohio to Washington, D.C. to demonstrate in favor of public works projects to help the unemployed. His march was joined by thousands of unemployed workers, and "Coxey's army" became a major worry to the authorities that a new revolution might be taking place. However, when Coxey arrived in Washington, D.C., he and the other leaders of the march were arrested for walking on the grass in front of the Capitol. "Coxey's army" quickly fell apart without any leadership, and any potential threat to the Republic was avoided.

Another mass movement that took place under this transit was the Pullman strike. The workers for the Pullman railroad car company went on strike to protest the feudal conditions under which they were forced to live. For the first time, other railroad workers around the country supported the strike by walking off the job, slowing down work, and even acts of sabotage. President Cleveland sent in Federal troops to crush the strike, but the event marked the beginning of national labor movements. As with Coxey's army, there was fear of revolution or civil war, but the intervention of the Federal government prevented wider discord and made the result seem anti-climactic.

How yellow are your journalists?

Eris was squaring the USA Mars in 1897, just as war fever was spreading over the country. William Randolph Hearst and his newspapers were busy fomenting a war with Spain over Cuba. The Hearst papers printed exaggerated stories about atrocities against Cuban freedom fighters. One notorious print showed a Cuban woman being strip-searched by male Spanish officials while on the deck of an American ship. Such stories brought out feelings of outraged chivalry in the American public. Only later was it revealed that the strip-search in question had been done by female officials in private.

By 1898, when Eris was in opposition to the USA Neptune, the public had been deluded into fighting "a splendid little war", as Secretary of State John Hay described it. The Spanish-American war did not have the same urgency or carnage as the American Revolution or the Civil War. In a conflict fought mainly overseas, there were images of military glory and patriotism, which dazzled the people, and made them ignore complaints about "imperialism." The public immediately mythologized the heroes of the war. Admiral George Dewey was seen as the hero of Manila Bay, though in truth his metal battleships were up against a small, wooden fleet. (Out of 5,859 shots fired, only 142 hit their targets, which showed the poor gunnery skills of the American fleet.) Theodore Roosevelt was immortalized for his charge up San Juan Hill, and he was forever depicted as a man on horseback. (In reality, the charge up San Juan Hill was done on foot because none of the Rough Riders had horses.) It was a war that inflated the American self image, and made people think in terms of the USA as being an "empire."

With the coming of the 20th century, Eris was trine the USA Mercury in 1905-1906. It was a time when journalism took a dramatic turn, and major exposures of corporations showed the seamy underside of business. Ida Tarbell, Upton Sinclair, and Lincoln Steffens inspired reform by writing about business practices that needed to be changed. Although President Theodore Roosevelt supported these changes, he referred to these journalists as "muckrakers", which he intended to be a slur because he thought they were focusing too much on the negative. The crusading journalists took "muckraker" as a compliment, and their work inspired a new generation of authors (Theodore Dreiser, Eugene O'Neill, Sinclair Lewis) to look at the darker side of life. Literature began examining gritty, naturalistic themes about impoverished lives, moral decay, and sex. The gentility of Victorian literature gave way to volumes of brutal themes.

From 1913-1919, Eris would be sextile the USA Pluto, and it was a time when the darkest forms of hysteria appeared on the American scene. Though the United States tried to stay neutral in World War I, stories about atrocities by the German army turned public opinion towards the Allies. When the Lusitania was sunk by a U-Boat in 1915, the American population was ready for war, but President Woodrow Wilson urged a diplomatic solution. In 1916, there was a threat of war with Mexico, when Pancho Villa raided the town of Columbus, New Mexico. General Pershing led a force into Mexico to capture Pancho Villa, but he was never caught. The retreat of the American forces prevented the outbreak of war with Mexico.

Wilson campaigned for re-election with the slogan, "He kept us out of war", but as soon as he was inaugurated, America was ready for war. The declaration of war in 1917 brought about anti-German hysteria. German food and beer were renamed. ("Sauerkraut" became "Liberty Cabbage.") Even the music of Beethoven was banned as "Hun music." The Federal government assumed more control over the lives of its citizens with a Draft to increase the military. A young lawyer named J. Edgar Hoover joined the government service and distinguished himself by organizing a round-up of males in the Manhattan area to check their Draft status.

As if war hysteria was not bad enough, the nation was subjected to Spanish Influenza, which ended up killing more people than World War One. Public gatherings were banned, and those going out in public were forced to wear surgical masks. Doctors were unable to find a cure, and the disease ravaged the Army camps that were tightly packed with new recruits. Officials speculated that if the disease continued unabated, the pandemic had the potential to wipe out the human race. Fortunately, by the autumn of 1918, the Spanish Influenza had run its course, and the numbers of deaths suddenly dropped.

To top the hysteria of war and influenza, the nation experienced its first great "Red Scare." On June 2, 1919, Attorney General A. Mitchell Palmer and Assistant Secretary of the Navy Franklin Roosevelt were almost killed by an anarchist bomb. This prompted the Attorney General to raid labor unions, left-wing political groups, and any organization that showed sympathy for the Bolshevik revolution in Russia. During the next two years, thousands of people would be arrested, and more than 500 would be deported to Russia. Although the press supported the Palmer raids, eventually the tide of public opinion would turn against Palmer when reports came of the spurious warrants, the abuse of police powers, and the disregard for civil liberties. Palmer would lose a chance for the Democratic Presidential nomination in 1920, and after all the hysteria the election would be won by Warren Harding, who promised a return to "Normalcy", which came with Prohibition and women voters.

Chapter 14
Rough and Ready Teddy

Natal Discord

Theodore Roosevelt hated being called "Teddy", but that was a term of endearment which millions of people used in referring to him. His name would be immortalized by the "Teddy Bear", a toy bear created to commemorate the fact that Roosevelt refused to kill a bear cub while on a hunting trip. (What is not remembered is that another member of the hunting party ended up killing the bear cub.) The toy bear captured the public imagination, and the result was that millions have been created over the years.

Roosevelt was born with Eris in the Tenth House conjunct his North Node, opposing his South Node, trine his Sun, and sextile his Pluto. His life was a whirlwind of contradictions that brought winds of change to the nation. He started life as an asthmatic invalid, but took up exercise and became a proponent of physical fitness. He was a hunter, but also a conservationist who developed the National Parks system. He promoted the glories of military conquest, but he was also the first American President to win the Nobel Peace Prize. He came from a patrician family, but showed a concern for the welfare of the lower classes, a cause that would be taken up by other Roosevelts.

Eris in Pisces

In the 1860's, Eris would conjunct Roosevelt's Part of Fortune, and there was a question as to whether he would survive his childhood. He needed to sleep sitting up so that his air passages would remain clear. Rather than be a helpless invalid, young Roosevelt was a hyperactive child, and his father helped him to channel that energy by having him take up boxing. Roosevelt also became interested in taxidermy, and by age nine he had a collection of preserved insects.

In the 1870's when Eris was quincunx his Saturn, the Roosevelt family made trips to Europe and the Middle East. Young Theodore was filled with a love for travel and adventure. By 1876, with Eris quincunx his Juno, Roosevelt was a Harvard man, nearly winning a boxing championship at the university. It was there that he developed his writing skills and began working on his first book, *The Naval War of 1812*.

As Eris squared his Vesta, Roosevelt went through some changes in his family life. In 1878, his father passed away. In 1880, he married Alice Hathaway and was happy with her for nearly four years. In 1884, when Eris was trine Roosevelt's Moon, Alice died from kidney failure after giving birth to their daughter, Alice. On the same day, Roosevelt's mother passed away. He would write in his diary, "The light has gone out of my life."

Roosevelt achieved solace by going West and setting up a ranch in the Dakotas. With Eris sextile his Mars, he threw himself into physical activity, taking up the life of a cowboy. The other cowboys quickly learned never to refer to Roosevelt as "four-eyes" after he knocked down one cowboy who dared to insult him. He became a deputy sheriff, and hunted down three outlaws who had stolen a boat. While marching them to jail, he managed to stay awake by reading a novel by Leo Tolstoy. His work helped him forget about his personal losses, and he began to focus on building a new life.

When Roosevelt had Eris squaring his Venus, he married for a second time to Edith Carow, a childhood friend. The couple honeymooned in Europe, where Roosevelt marked the Eris sextile Mars transit by climbing Mont Blanc. For this action, he was made

Theodore Roosevelt
October 27, 1858
7:45 pm LMT
New York, NY
Koch 40N42'52"
74W00'23"

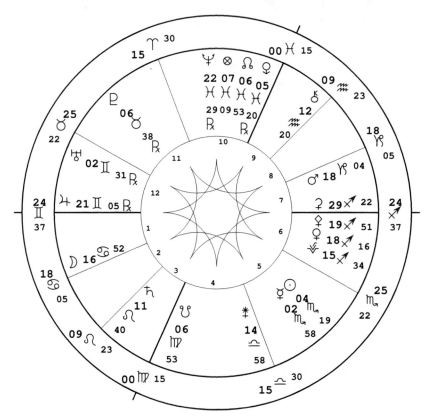

a member of the British Royal Society, a leading scientific body. Upon his return to the U.S.A., Roosevelt would continue with his love of politics.

In the 1890's, with Eris squaring his Pallas, Roosevelt was appointed to the Civil Service Commission. His great work there was undoing the influence of the "Spoils System" developed by Andrew Jackson. Government jobs would be held by qualified men instead of political hacks. Although appointed by President Benjamin Harrison, Roosevelt was so effective in his work that he was reappointed when President Grover Cleveland took office again.

Because of his work with the Civil Service Commission and his later work as Police Commissioner of New York City, Roosevelt became a rising star in national politics. When Eris was square his Jupiter in 1897, Roosevelt became Assistant Secretary of the Navy. He was a leading advocate for war against Spain in order to liberate Cuba. In 1898, when Eris was conjunct his Neptune, he began his legendary career as a warrior. As soon as war with Spain was declared, he sent orders to Admiral Dewey to capture Manila Bay in the Philippines. (This was done without consulting the Secretary of the Navy.) Roosevelt then resigned from the Navy Department and formed the Rough Riders, a collection of cowboys, prizefighters, and adventurers who would serve under him in Cuba.

Although the Rough Riders were supposed to be a cavalry unit, they arrived in Cuba without horses, because there were not enough transport ships. Only Roosevelt had a horse, but his famous charges up Kettle Hill and San Juan Hill were made on foot.

Roosevelt would call his charge up San Juan Hill, "the greatest day of my life." He was nominated for a Medal of Honor, but he never received it, possibly due to political machinations of his rivals. For the rest of his life, his friends would refer to him as "Colonel Roosevelt" in deference to his military success.

In the Spanish-American war, more soldiers died from malaria than from battle wounds. It was not a glamorous image in the history of warfare. Roosevelt's victories helped boost his public image, and he was seen as a gallant military figure. In 1898, he became Governor of New York, against the wishes of the political bosses. Thomas Platt, the leading political boss of New York, maneuvered the 1900 Republican convention so that Roosevelt would receive a nomination for Vice-President, considered to be a politically dead-end job. Roosevelt's position would take a dramatic turn in 1901 with the assassination of President William McKinley, making Roosevelt the youngest President in the history of the nation.

Although he promised to continue McKinley's policies, Roosevelt began his administration by "trust-busting." He had Congress pass laws restricting the powers of major corporations. These actions were so popular with the general public that Roosevelt was re-elected in 1904. Once he had won the Presidency on his own, Roosevelt moved ahead with more sweeping reform.

During his second term in office, Roosevelt had Eris squaring his Ascendant. It would become his time of greatest achievement. He negotiated a peace settlement between Russia and Japan, which ended the Russo-Japanese war, and earned him the Nobel Peace Prize. He authorized construction of the Panama Canal, and became the first sitting President to leave the country while in office to visit the canal construction site. After reading *The Jungle* by Upton Sinclair, he signed the Meat Inspection Act, and later the Pure Food and Drug Act. The good publicity his administration enjoyed may have been due to his considerate treatment of reporters. When he saw reporters huddled outside of the White House, waiting for news in a cold rain storm, Roosevelt set aside a room in the White House for reporters to congregate, thereby creating the White House Press Corps.

Roosevelt could have been re-elected in 1908, but he decided to leave office when his popularity was high, and he chose William Howard Taft as his successor. Roosevelt went off on a safari to Africa, and when he returned to America he was disappointed to find that Taft had not continued his progressive policies. Roosevelt would challenge Taft for the Presidency in 1912, but his "Bull Moose" ticket would end up losing the Presidency to Woodrow Wilson.

Roosevelt's health declined after an arduous river exploration in South America up "the River of Doubt", which was later named "Rio Teodoro" in his honor. He nearly died from malaria and an infection in his leg. Though he wanted to lead American troops in World War I, Roosevelt was considered to be too old and in poor condition. He did help the war effort by recruiting and selling war bonds. He even took time to criticize Woodrow Wilson, saying that Americans still had a right to criticize a President, even in wartime. It was expected that Roosevelt would become the Republican nominee in 1920.

On January 6, 1919, Roosevelt died in his sleep from heart failure. Vice-President Thomas Marshall said of his passing, "Death had to take Roosevelt in his sleep, because if he had been awake, there would have been a fight." After his death, Roosevelt achieved an apotheosis like Washington and Lincoln. A decade later, when Eris had moved into Aries, and was sextile Roosevelt's Uranus and quincunx his Mercury, his face was chosen to be put on Mount Rushmore, placed right between Jefferson and Lincoln.

In 2001, when Eris was square Roosevelt's Mars and trine his Venus, Congress finally voted to award Theodore Roosevelt a Medal of Honor for his military exploits more than a hundred years earlier. So far he is the only President to be honored with the highest military award. The medal was placed on display at the Roosevelt Room in the White House.

Chapter 15

"That Man in the White House"

When Franklin Delano Roosevelt started his political career, he seemed like a clone of his fifth cousin, Theodore Roosevelt. Both were Harvard graduates who had traveled extensively, and who got their political start in New York politics. Since Theodore Roosevelt wore a pince-nez, Franklin had to wear a pince-nez as well. Both were athletic men, but Franklin's course in life would take a more dramatic personal turn than Theodore would ever experience.

FDR was born into a world of wealth and privilege and was indulged by an overprotective mother. Eris was sextile his Jupiter during his youth in the 1880's, and he started life with a yearning for sports and travel. His father was emotionally remote, and much too old for playing with his young son. Young Franklin might have grown up to be a spoiled society playboy had not other influences acted upon the course of his life.

Eris in Pisces

FDR's first brush with destiny came in 1888, when Eris was opposing his Uranus and sextile his Chiron. His father took him to Washington, D.C. to meet President Grover Cleveland. The President greeted young Franklin with the words, "Young man,

I am going to make a strange wish for you. I wish that you never grow up to become President of the United States." Years later, when burdened by the difficulties of the Presidency, FDR would understand the meaning of Cleveland's wish.

The greatest influence on FDR's life would come when he was sent to attend Groton Academy, run by Rev. Endicott Peabody. It was the belief of Rev. Peabody that Christians had a duty to help those who were less fortunate, and he encouraged his students to enter public service. FDR would later say of Rev. Peabody, "As long as I live his influence will mean more to me than that of any other people next to my father and mother." From Groton Academy, FDR would go on to Harvard, while Eris was squaring his Midheaven. He became the President of "The Harvard Crimson" newspaper, and lived in luxurious quarters as a member of the Alpha Delta Phi fraternity.

In 1902, as Eris entered his Seventh House and was sextile his Pallas, FDR met his fifth cousin, Eleanor Roosevelt at a White House reception. The outgoing Franklin became interested in the shy Eleanor. When he announced his intention to marry her, he got stern opposition from his mother. However, the wedding did take place in 1905, with President Theodore Roosevelt giving away the bride.

The marriage of Eleanor and Franklin, though it seemed successful at the beginning, was a difficult sham. Eleanor disliked sex, and was burdened by giving birth to five children. She did not socialize as well as Franklin. He began a series of affairs, starting with Eleanor's social secretary, Lucy Mercer, then with his secretary, Missy Lehand, and even during World War Two there were rumors that he was having an affair with Princess Martha of Norway. Eleanor stayed with Franklin for political purposes, and she eventually became more extroverted as she got involved with social causes. They would lead separate lives, but they would be joined by a love of political power.

During World War I, FDR had Eris sextile his Pluto and squaring his Mars. After years of involvement in New York politics, he was given the post of Assistant Secretary of the Navy, which had been held by Theodore Roosevelt. It enabled FDR to

This photograph of FDR
as a young man shows
marked family resemblance
to Theodore Roosevelt.

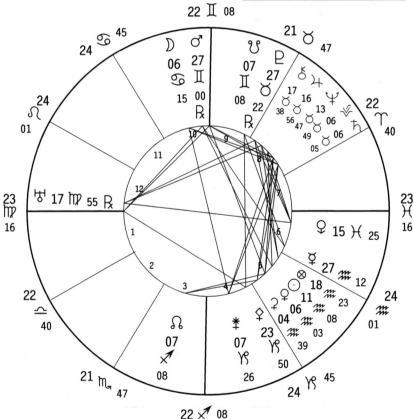

Franklin D. Roosevelt
January 30, 1882 8:45 pm LMT
Hyde Park, NY
Koch 41N47'05" 73W56'01"

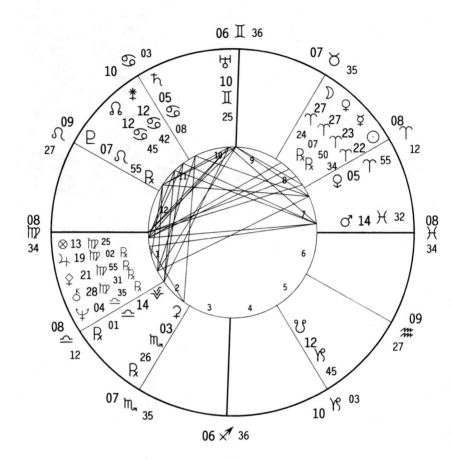

FDR Death
April 12, 1945
3:35 pm CWT, Warm Springs, GA
Koch 32N53'25" 84W40'52"

be seen on the stage of national politics, and promote his career. This was also the time when Eleanor discovered that Franklin was having an affair with Lucy Mercer. Eleanor was willing to divorce Franklin so he could marry Lucy Mercer, but Lucy rejected that idea because she was a Roman Catholic who could not marry a divorced man.

Maintaining the image of a successful politician, FDR became the Democratic Vice-Presidential nominee in 1920. Running with Ohio Governor James Cox, FDR supported the internationalist policies of Woodrow Wilson. The Democrats ended up losing to Warren Harding and Calvin Coolidge, who promised a return to "Normalcy", whatever that was.

For FDR "Normalcy" was about to come to an end as he contracted polio and lost the use of his legs. For years he would struggle against the illness, finding that the hydrotherapy in Warm Springs, GA provided the best relief. As Eris moved into Aries, FDR maintained his political career by deftly concealing his handicap. Through the cooperation of reporters, Roosevelt was never shown in a wheelchair nor walking with braces.

Eris in Aries

By the time of the Great Depression, FDR was fully involved in politics and had become Governor of New York. His promotion of social programs to help the downtrodden caught the public imagination, and he was elected President in a landslide.

His "New Deal" programs provided work for the unemployed and set up regulations to help working people. His regulation of the business class caused many of the wealthy to refer to him as "a traitor to his class", and they were filled with such a hatred of him that they could only refer to him as "that man in the White House."

In the late 1930's, Eris was sextile his Ceres, and FDR had won a reputation as a nurturing individual who cared about the common man. There were difficulties with his policies, such as when the Supreme Court declared parts of the New Deal to be unconstitutional. When FDR tried to add more justices to the Supreme Court, he was denounced as a dictator trying to "pack" the Court and subvert one of the branches of government. His critics pointed out that his policies had not done enough to restore prosperity to businesses.

Though the economy was still weak, the fact that someone in the government had shown concern for the working class brought FDR an enhanced image. His "Fireside Chats" addressed people, by way of radio, in a plain and comforting manner. Because of this empathy, the public was willing to break the historical standard that a President should only have two terms. In 1940, FDR was elected for an unprecedented third term. His leadership during World War II would be so effective, he would receive a fourth term.

Unfortunately, FDR died before the war ended. At the time of his death by cerebral hemorrhage, Eris was conjunct the Eighth House cusp, sextile the Midheaven, square Saturn, trine Pluto, quincunx Ceres, and opposing Neptune. His passing would be a time for grief in most of the world, save for the Axis powers. In Great Britain, the level of national mourning was comparable to the passing of a monarch. In America, his passing would be likened to a casualty of war, and some newspapers listed Roosevelt's name at the top of the listings of the war dead. As the news was being released to the world, Roosevelt's family and friends were busy covering up the fact that he had been visiting with his former mistress, Lucy Mercer, shortly before he died.

In 1946, Eris would be sextile his Venus. Some of the social programs he worked for would be swept away at the end of the war as being nothing more than "bureaucracy." As Republicans regained control of Congress, they denigrated the New Deal as being "Socialist" and said that "Communists" had been allowed into government. Yet, the people never stopped loving FDR, and as a tribute to him, his likeness was put on the dime, as an acknowledgement of his work for the "March of Dimes" campaign against polio.

In 1997, when Eris was sextile FDR's Part of Fortune, a memorial to him was dedicated in Washington, D.C. The creation of the FDR statue stirred a bit of discord, because the artist wanted to depict FDR seated, enfolded by a large cape. Advocates for the handicapped wanted FDR depicted in a wheelchair, thereby symbolizing the conquering of his disability. A compromise was reached in that wheelchair casters were placed at the back of the statue, just beneath the cape, to suggest that FDR was sitting on a wheelchair.

Chapter 16
America's Dictator

Natal Discord

With Eris trine Uranus, J. Edgar Hoover set himself up as the main opponent of every progressive movement during his lifetime. Whether the subject was civil rights, labor unions, or the peace movement, Hoover's response was always the same. He would accuse them of being filled with Communists, and attempting to spread Communist doctrines across the land. Whenever anyone suggested Hoover was being paranoid, he would respond that Communists were trying to destroy the FBI in order to infiltrate the government.

Eris was sextile Hoover's Venus, and he had a very unusual relationship. Until 1938, he lived with his mother. After her death, he was always in the company of Clyde Tolson, the number two man at the FBI. They would constantly dine together, visit the racetrack together, and go on vacations together. Although they would both be offended if anyone suggested that they appeared to be in a homosexual relationship, by all outward appearances they looked like a Gay couple totally devoted to each other.

Eris in Pisces

Hoover was raised as a Presbyterian and was trained with the moral certitude of that faith. For a while, he considered becoming a minister. With transiting Eris squaring his Juno, he was very devoted to his faith and family. He also took up football, tennis, and golf, and pursued them with an aggressive enthusiasm, but then he dropped the sports when he found he could not master them.

In 1908, when Eris was conjunct Hoover's North Node, opposing his South Node and squaring his Vesta, an event took place in Hoover's home town that would effect the course of his life. Attorney General Charles Bonaparte (distant nephew of Napoleon) lobbied Congress for the creation of a Bureau of Investigation in the Justice department. The members of Congress balked at the idea, fearing it would turn into a national secret police organization. Bonaparte assured them that the Bureau of Investigation would be used to investigate interstate crime. With that assurance, Congress allowed the Bureau to come into existence.

By 1917, Hoover had received a law degree from George Washington University. He went into government service, and entered the Justice Department as a clerk. With Eris trine his Pallas and squaring his Jupiter, Hoover approached his duties with fanatical devotion. He would take on all work, accepting small tasks, and would gladly work overtime. His efforts impressed his superiors, especially the way he kept file cards on suspected subversives during the post-war period.

Eris in Aries

Due to his devoted work ethic, Hoover was chosen to head the Bureau of Investigation in 1924. He immediately set about housecleaning and raising the standards of the bureau. Previously, agents had been cheap detectives with shady pasts. Hoover insisted that all agents had to be college graduates with a degree in law. They had to wear neat suits (no red ties) and hats. Later, when hats went out of fashion, the FBI agents still had to wear them, making them obvious during undercover investigations.

In the 1930's, when gangs of bank robbers began oper-

J. Edgar Hoover
January 1, 1895
7:30 am EST
Washington, DC
Koch 38N53'42" 77W02'12"

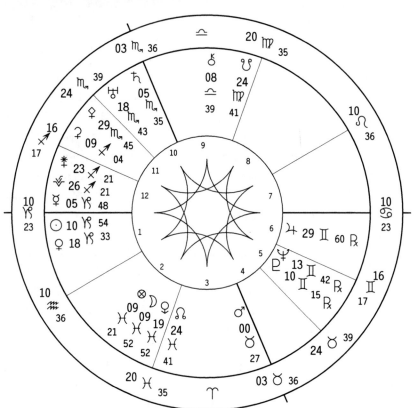

ating around the country, the Bureau became involved with the interstate pursuit of the gangsters. Hoover began a major public relations blitz, impressing upon the public that the Bureau was taking the lead in law enforcement. As a result, the Bureau was given more authority and was officially re-christened the Federal Bureau of Investigation. Hoover attained a reputation of being American's Number One Lawman, always maintaining a pure profile, even though he was often gambling and visiting night-clubs.

Yet, there were disturbing trends emerging from FBI activities. When Postmaster General James Farley suggested another person should be made head of the FBI, Hoover ordered agents to keep surveillance on Farley, to the point of tapping his phone and following him down the street. When agents reported that they could not find any dirt on Farley, Hoover ordered them to start investigating Farley's friends.

In 1942, with Eris square Hoover's Mercury and quincunx his Saturn, the FBI scored one of its biggest cases by arresting eight Nazi saboteurs who had been brought to America by U-Boat. The case was trumpeted as a triumph for the FBI, and sent fear through the hearts of potential Fifth Columnists. The FBI was considered to be so powerful, the Germans never tried landing agents again. It was only long after the war that it was revealed that the case had been broken when one saboteur turned himself in and informed on the others. In fact, the informant was nearly chased away from FBI headquarters, until he revealed that he was carrying a briefcase full of money.

Once the Nazi menace had been crushed, J. Edgar Hoover turned his investigations to ferreting out Communists. By the 1950's, when Eris was opposing his Chiron and trine his Ceres, he was considered to be the epitome of a loyal American, using his influence to locate Communists. (At the time, it was estimated the American Communist Party had one FBI infiltrator for every five members.) Hoover made cameo appearances in movies, had numerous magazine articles written about his work, and even made an appearance in a *Dennis the Menace* comic book. All of this helped create a cult of personality, particularly within the FBI, where Hoover ruled over his agents with an iron hand. Agents could be transferred or fired for the slightest infraction, even shaking hands with Hoover with wet palms.

By the 1960's, when Eris was square his Sun and sextile Pluto, disturbing stories started coming out about Hoover's activities in the FBI. There were reports that he was using agents to do yard work and make repairs on his house. Black agents were assigned to be his chauffeurs. There were stories about secret files that contained the foibles and peccadilloes of Congressmen, Senators, and many celebrities. It seemed that a sign of fame in America was to have J. Edgar Hoover open a file.

Former FBI agent William Turner described the sort of power that Hoover developed over the years:

"Difficult as it is to believe, Hoover took over during the Calvin Coolidge administration in 1924. So entrenched has he become that he considers presidents mere transients. He was given a free hand in molding his agency, and the FBI reflects to an uncommon degree his own personality. His whims, fancies, prejudices, and idiosyncrasies are stamped on it, and his slightest wish, expressed or implied becomes an edict to his subordinates. One amusing but quite true story will illustrate the point. The Director is fond of jotting pungent notations on the borders of memorandums, and the filling of all four borders is known as a 'four-bagger.' Once, he was irked by a memo that left little room for his scrawlings. 'Watch the borders,' he wrote in his characteristic green ink. Uncertain of what he meant and afraid to ask, officials carried out the dictum to the letter. For over a week, agents were staked out along the Canadian and Mexican borders, unsure of what they were watching for." [1]

Hoover developed an uneasy working relationship with the Kennedys, resenting Robert Kennedy's authority as Attorney General. Hoover despised the civil rights movement and referred to Martin Luther King Jr. as "the most notorious liar in the country." [2] Hoover maintained surveillance on King, and started a poison-pen campaign against the civil rights leader, hoping to force him into suicide with the threats of potentially damning information.

Hoover also kept insisting that organized crime did not exist, even when state authorities turned up evidence proving the contrary. He refused to go after Mafia bosses, leading to speculation that he was somehow under their power. One sleazy rumor was that the Mafia bosses had gotten photographs of Hoover in a compromising position with Clyde Tolson. In spite of Hoover's lack of investigation, he still remained at the peak of his power in the agency.

In 1965, when he reached his 70th birthday, a special order was signed by President Lyndon Johnson, allowing Hoover to remain at his job way past the retirement age. No one could imagine another person at the head of the FBI. The cult of personality was too strong, and those who attained high positions in the Bureau owed their allegiance directly to Hoover. If any political figure dared to question Hoover's tactics, other political figures could be found to rush to Hoover's defense.

On May 2, 1972, the body of J. Edgar Hoover was found in his house, and the cause of death was listed as high blood pressure. Eris was sextile Hoover's Neptune, and his image of a great leader was maintained to the end. His body was allowed to lie in state in the Capitol Rotunda, and he was given a Masonic funeral. After his death, stories would leak out about the strange activities of the FBI because of Hoover's demands.

Endnote:

[1] Turner, William W., *Hoover's FBI*, Dell Publishing Company, New York, 1971, Page xi

[2] Ibid, page 82

Part IV

Eris in Aries:

Rambunctious

Eris entered Aries in 1924, but did not aspect the USA chart until 1930 when it was square the USA Venus. Although it was the time of the Great Depression, it was also a time of people coming together to help others through the crisis. In 1936, Hugh Morris, author of *The Art of Kissing* wrote, "According to released figures, there were more children born during the depression than there had been in the good times. This means that, although married people did not have money, they still had themselves. They still had love." [1]

Groups of farmers banded together to fight for higher prices for farm goods, and to buy up foreclosed farms for the sake of their previous owners. Evicted persons in the cities banded together in shanty-towns called "Hoovervilles", which became cooperative communities, with people bartering services between themselves. In 1932, World War I veterans joined a "Bonus Army" to demand help from the government, but were chased out of Washington D.C. by the regular army.

How Now Brown Dow?

Although the Stock Market Crash of 1929 marked the beginning of the Great Depression, the influence of Eris can best be seen in an event which marked the nadir of the decline. On July 8, 1932, the Dow Jones Industrial Average hit the lowest point in its history with 40.56. The chart for this event shows Eris conjunct the Descendant, trine the Part of Fortune, and sextile Saturn, marking the collapse of Dow Jones into the crapper. However, with Eris square Venus and the Midheaven and opposing the Ascendant, Dow Jones would only go up after this, and it managed to finish the day at 41.22. With Eris quincunx Neptune, some people would buy into the idea that "prosperity is around the corner." The Dow Jones Industrial Average would not return to its 1929 levels of prosperity until 1954.

With the inauguration of Franklin Delano Roosevelt, the spirit of cooperation and coming together was played out in the New Deal. Unemployed workers were organized into camps to take part in public works programs. Roosevelt's critics denounced the New Deal programs as "alphabet soup", but they caught on with the public and provided relief at a time when many felt they had been forgotten.

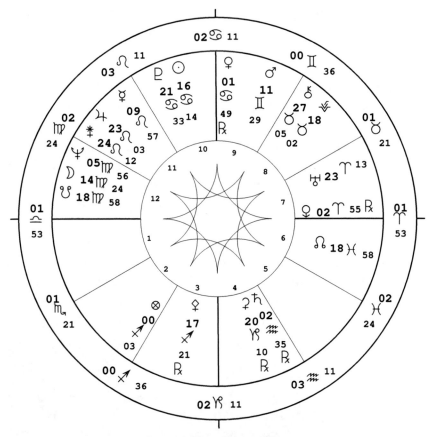

Dow Jones Worst Day
July 8, 1932, 12:00 noon EDT
New York, NY
Koch 40N42'51" 74W00'22"

It was also a time when labor unions were empowered, due to the Wagner Act which created a National Labor Relations Board.

Recovery from the Great Depression did not take place for several years, and the Depression was declared to be over in 1941, just as Eris was squaring the USA Jupiter. The approach of World War II brought a tremendous period of economic growth to the USA, as war industries started booming. With the men going off to fight as soldiers, women started taking jobs in the war plants. With all of the overtime work, there were plenty of savings accounts, providing capital for future investment. The most beneficial result of the war was the GI Bill, which provided college degrees and homes to the returning veterans, known as "The Greatest Generation".

Pearl Harbor

When World War II began in 1939, the majority of Americans wanted to remain neutral. Though the war in Europe saw many Nazi victories, and though Franklin Roosevelt promoted Lend-Lease for the British, there was still a national reluctance to commit troops. The "America First" organization spread isolationist views, until an event took place that would galvanize the entire nation and get Americans involved in the World War.

In the days before December 7, 1941, Eris was trine Mercury, and there were indications that something was about to happen, but no one could piece the puzzle together. American cryptographers intercepted a message written in the Japanese diplomatic code, which instructed the Japanese envoys in

Photo taken just after the attack on Pearl Harbor

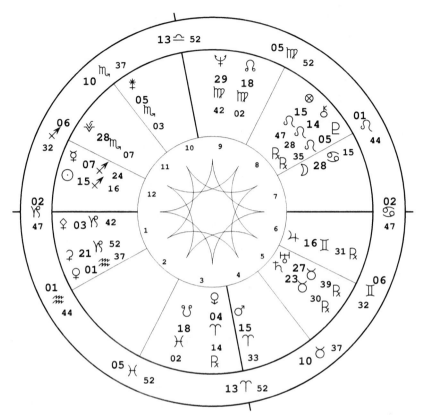

The Attack on Pearl Harbor
December 7, 1941, 7:48 am HST
Honolulu, Hawaii
Koch 21N18'25" 157W51'30"

Washington D.C. to break off negotiations. This message would not be decoded until it was too late. Two Japanese midget submarines were destroyed by American warships near Pearl Harbor, but no general alarm was made. Incoherent radio messages came in from American planes patrolling around Oahu. The planes quickly disappeared. A radar station detected a large squadron of incoming aircraft, but the technicians, unfamiliar with the new technology, thought it was only a flock of birds.

At 7:48 am, the first Japanese attack hit Kaneohe Air Base. Eris in the Third House was sextile Venus in the First House and trine Pluto in the Eighth House. The attack became a disaster for American sailors in cruisers and battleships. Hundreds were killed in a matter of minutes as explosions devastated the ships and caused capsizing. Airplanes were bombed on the ground, depriving the American forces of air cover. Within ninety minutes, more than 2000 servicemen would be dead, and 18 ships would be sunk or run aground.

In spite of the terrible surprise attack, with Eris square the Ascendant and Pallas, American forces managed to keep their discipline. The USS Nevada was able to get underway and tried to get out of the harbor. Because of attacks by Japanese planes, the commanding officer decided to beach the battleship rather than risk having it sunk at the entrance to the harbor. The destroyer USS Alwyn was able to get out of the harbor and operate at sea. By the time the second Japanese wave came over, Americans were able to get their anti-aircraft batteries operating. This convinced the Japanese not to try a third wave. Because of this, the Americans were able to save their oil tanks and the submarine pens, which enabled them to be able to strike back against the Japanese sooner than expected.

With Eris quincunx Juno, the attack on Pearl Harbor united America against the Japanese. When Germany and Italy declared war on America three days later, the country was committed to fighting the Axis powers. It would take four years of military and industrial commitment to provide the result of the occupation of Europe, and then the occupation of Japan, after surrender was prompted by the atomic bomb attacks. After Pearl Harbor, America would never again think of being isolationist, and would design foreign policy befitting a leading world power.

Hiroshima

The American development of the atomic bomb began as a response to stories that Nazi Germany was working on a similar weapon. When Germany was invaded, it was discovered that German scientists had not gotten very far with the weapon. The Manhattan Project still continued, and it was expected that the atomic bomb would play a part in the invasion of Japan. General George Marshall thought that the atomic bomb could be used to clear the

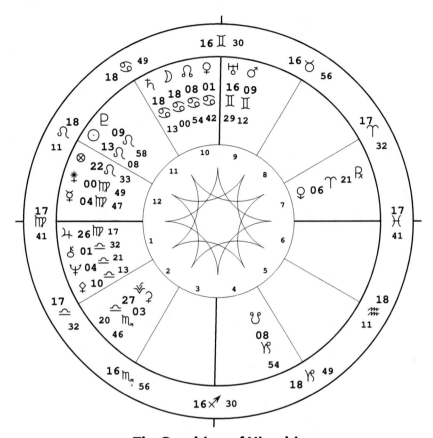

The Bombing of Hiroshima
August 6, 1945, 8:15 am JST
Hiroshima, Japan
Koch 34N24 132E27

beaches before an invasion force arrived in Japan. However, the scientists who developed the bomb decided that a city should be the first target. Hiroshima was chosen because it was a major communications center and had military headquarters and bases.

On August 6, 1945, Eris was sextile Mars and trine Pluto, and the destruction of Hiroshima would change the rules of warfare. Military victories had been won with armies clashing, and soldiers winning through force of numbers or superior strategy. With the coming of nuclear warfare, the world was seeing weapons that could not be fought against, and a single weapon would bring total devastation to an area. With the speed of flashing light, more people would die in a few seconds than had died in many of the long, drawn out battles of history.

With Eris quincunx Mercury, word of the explosion became major news around the world. Throughout America, the detonation was received with expressions of jubilation, with the public seeing the atomic bomb as the weapon that would end the war. With Eris opposing Neptune and Pallas, many hoped that the atomic bomb would be the weapon that would end all warfare, and no nation would want to attack America with such a weapon ready for retaliation. A bomb that could destroy an entire city had seemed like something out of science fiction, but now had become science fact.

Eris was square the North and South Node at the time of the attack, and the South Node was conjunct the point of natal Eris in the USA chart. There was a feeling of national pride with this weapon, and a sense of relief that millions of soldiers would not have to risk their lives storming the beaches of Japan. Yet, the atomic bomb became America's golden apple of discord, because it created an inflated image that America was the most powerful of all nations, and some persons wanted to drop atomic bombs on other nations, such as Russia, just to maintain that grandiose self-worth.

With Eris quincunx Ceres, after a while stories began to leak out about the horrible burn victims and the terrors of radiation sickness. People began questioning the value of atomic warfare. Images of the charred victims added to the fears of the post-war era, particularly when Russia developed its own atomic bomb. There arose a "ban the bomb" movement, which sought to warn people about the devastation of nuclear warfare. Unfortunately, their message would be drowned out by the Cold War rhetoric of maintaining nuclear superiority and the need to close the missile gap.

As terrible as the Hiroshima bombing was, the conclusion of World War II could have been far worse without the atomic bomb. In July, 1945, before the atomic bomb was revealed, the U.S. Army conducted a feasibility study for using poison gas during the invasion of Japan. The plan was to fire poison gas shells into major ports such as Tokyo, Yokohama, and Nagasaki, and then just sail in the American fleet once the poison gas had cleared the harbor. Casualty estimates for this tactic were in the range of five million civilian dead. It could have become America's equivalent of the Holocaust, and would have ruined America's reputation for leadership in the postwar world.

Is Your Mommy a Commie?

By 1945, Eris was sextile the USA South Node and trine the USA North Node. After the war, there was a period of economic decline, and a questioning of American values. During the war, there had been an ideal of spreading freedom throughout the world. After the war, the focus shifted away from "pro-freedom" to "anti-communism." Fear of Communism would lead to a panic in the government, with workers, politicians, and even soldiers being hounded for their political beliefs. Smear campaigns with late-night phone calls and doctored photographs became the new tactic, and people started to wonder if America had lost its soul. The ugly side of these new tactics was embodied in Senator Joseph McCarthy, who indulged in personal attacks and guilt by innuendo.

The influence of McCarthy came to an end in 1954, when Eris was squaring the USA Eris, quincunx the USA Ascendant, and sextile the USA Uranus. A new force in the land, television, focused its eye on the happenings in government. The confrontation between McCarthy and attorney Joseph Welch on national television opened the eyes of the public to the sort of bullying behavior McCarthy had displayed. Attacks by journalists such as Drew Pearson and Edward R. Murrow also showed up the abuses of McCarthy's tactics. His influence quickly declined and he was soon to die as a political non-entity. With the passing of the "red scare", the nation entered a halcyon period, marked by the ever increasing number of TV antennas on rooftops.

In the turbulent 1960's, Eris entered the Sixth House of the USA chart. At first, the motto of the decade would be found in John F. Kennedy's words, "Ask not what your country can do for you. Ask what you can do for your country." This brought a spirit of volunteerism in the Peace Corps and other government programs. Medicare and additional welfare programs were signed into law, providing services for needy citizens. By the late 1960's there would be questions about the spirit of service, as the Vietnam War continued without an end in sight.

How Civil are Your Rights?

Perhaps the most beneficial change in the 1960's was the signing of the Civil Rights Act on July 2, 1964, which was to end segregation in America. Eris was conjunct the Moon, and it was a moment of great emotional concern for everyone. With Eris square the Sun, the Civil Rights Act was seen as an affirmation of the statement in the Declaration of Independence that "all men are created equal." It was an example of the nation living up to its ideals, and doing away with the negative legacy of Jim Crow laws.

However, Eris was also sextile Mars, and for the racist groups that promoted segregation, this act was seen as a call to arms to promote States Rights. For the black population it served as a call to mobilize, and sometime militarize in the support of voting rights. There would be marches and sometimes riots as communities would rise up against repression. In many cases, resisting repression was met with more repression, as racist groups would resort to murder to suppress those who advocated voting rights.

With Eris quincunx Pluto in the Twelfth House, there would be federal investigations of groups performing racial violence, leading to convictions and a realization that the Federal government was going to back up the Civil Rights Act. With Eris quincunx Neptune, the legislation was seen as an attempt to live up to the transformational vision of the nation, best expressed by Martin Luther King, Jr. in his "I have a dream" speech.

The non-violent efforts of Dr. King came to an end on April 4, 1968. Eris on the Descendant was conjunct the Sun and Saturn, opposing the Ascendant, and quincunx Juno. The assassination of Dr. King would bring the issues of Civil Rights to the forefront, forging new alliances as people would be united in their grief. As with the death of John F. Kennedy, people wondered about a conspiracy and whether evil forces running a shadow government were at work.

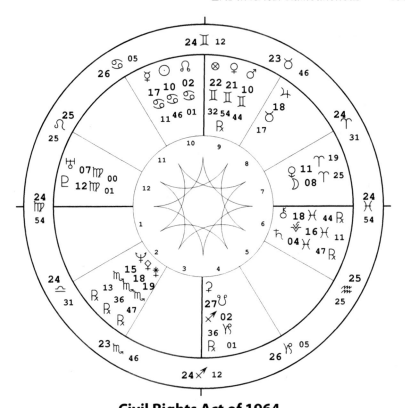

Civil Rights Act of 1964
July 2, 1964, 12:00pm EDT
Washington DC
Koch 38N53'42" 77W02'12"

The fear of conspiracy would increase in June with the assassination of Robert F. Kennedy. In the event chart, Eris was conjunct Vesta, marking upheaval in a family that seemed to be cursed by the loss of so many promising children. Eris was sextile Venus and the Sun, signaling the connection of feelings that millions felt over the tragedy of having a potential leader cut down. Once again, the killer would be a "lone gunman" and there was further speculation of conspiracy against candidates who were working for the interests of the people.

Violent protest against the Vietnam war and racial issues shocked the country and made people wonder if another revolution was going to take place. The Democratic leadership

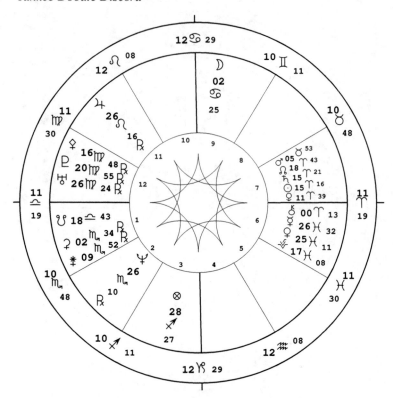

Martin Luther King Assassination
April 4, 1968, 6:01pm CST
Memphis, TN
Koch 35N08'58" 90W02'56"

did not seem capable of preventing a violent overthrow. In fear of such a change, voters turned to a "law and order" candidate who promised to get crime off the streets. (Little did anyone think where it would end up!)

Drowning in Watergate

Eris squaring the USA Sun marked the downfall of President Richard Nixon and proved that the legal system worked. Starting in June 1972, the Watergate scandal revealed the level of corruption in the Executive branch of government, with a secret security force ("The Plumbers") performing illegal surveillance. Nixon's justification would be, "If the President does it, it's not illegal."[2]

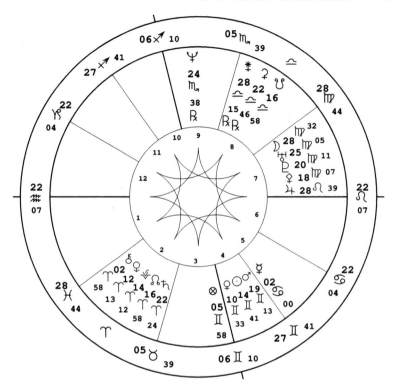

Robert Kennedy Assassination
June 5, 1968, 0:15am PDT
Los Angeles, CA
Koch 34N03'08" 118W14'34"

The public was not buying that reasoning, and by 1974 Nixon was forced to resign in order to escape impeachment. Watergate entered the history books as a Constitutional crisis and the closest the country came to tyranny.

In the chart for Nixon's resignation (on page 163), Eris in the Sixth House is trine the Sun in the Tenth House, indicating a sore spot to the national image. Eris is trine the North Node, and sextile the South Node, leading to a question of values that would bring such a change. However, with Eris squaring Saturn, there was a sense of relief that the worst was over, and there would be an end to the "stonewalling" that had hampered the government. With Uranus and Vesta on the Ascendant, there was hope that the new administration of Gerald Ford would bring new prospects, but with the Void-of-Course Moon sitting on the Descendant, Watergate would still haunt the new administration, particularly after Ford's pardon of Nixon.

In the reaction to Watergate, an outsider, Jimmy Carter, was elected President in 1976. As Eris opposed the USA Saturn, Carter began a restructuring of American foreign policy, based on human rights and diplomacy instead of military intervention. The goal was to raise America's moral character in the eyes of the world. This was partly accomplished through the Camp David Accords between Israel and Egypt. However, Carter's administration foundered with the Iranian hostage crisis, and the voters came to look at diplomacy as a form of weakness, resulting in Carter's defeat in 1980. More than twenty years later, Carter's methods of diplomacy would be vindicated when he received the Nobel Peace Prize.

In 1986, as Eris was trine the USA Midheaven, another scandal broke which threatened the reputation of the government. Colonel Oliver North was discovered to be running a "shadow government" in the basement of the White House. Arms were being sold to Iran, and the profits from the sales were being used to fund the Nicaraguan Contras.

The Iran-Contra scandal made people question who was running the country, and what accountability they had. Many of the leaders were able to escape prosecution by saying, "I don't remember" or "I was out of the loop", making it seem like they really were not the ones running the country. Further discord was added with the news that President Reagan was consulting an astrologer about official matters, and his opponents suggested that he was not mentally all there.

With the collapse of the Soviet Union, it was hoped that there would be an end to discord once the Cold War fears had disappeared. However, new tensions were raised in American foreign policy with increased involvement in the Middle East. The Gulf War quickly demonstrated American military might at work, defeating one of the largest armies in the area with the liberation of Kuwait and the breaking of the influence of Iraq. Yet, the presence

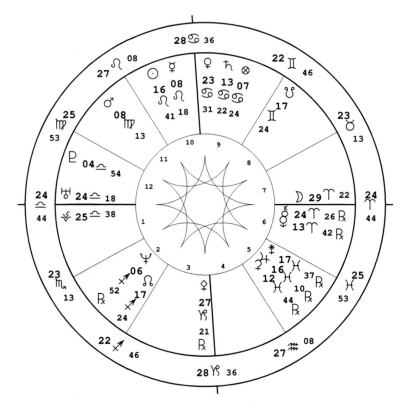

Nixon Resignation
Aug. 9, 1974, 12:00pm EDT
Washington, D.C.
Koch 38N53'42" 77W02'12"

of American troops in Saudi Arabia, and the continued support of Israel would cause a backlash against America.

On February 26, 1993, a truck bomb exploded in the parking garage under the North Tower of the World Trade Center. The chart for this event shows Eris conjunct Venus, trine Chiron and the North Node, sextile the South Node and Pallas, opposing Jupiter, and squaring the Uranus-Neptune conjunction. The terrorists responsible hoped to cause the North Tower to collapse and fall into the South Tower, causing hundreds of thousands of deaths. Six people were killed and more than a thousand were injured in the attack, mostly due to smoke inhalation.

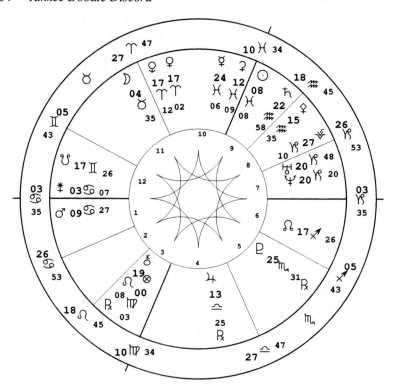

World Trade Center Bombing 1993
February 26, 1993   12:18pm EST
New York, NY
Koch 40N42'51" 74W00'23"

The attack was intended as a high-profile statement for a terrorist organization denouncing America's support of Israel. FBI investigators were able to local an axle that had been part of the deadly truck, and they got a vehicle identification number that allowed them to trace the truck to a rental center in New Jersey. The man who rented the truck had reported it stolen, and when he returned to the rental agency to get a refund on his deposit, he was arrested by the FBI. This brought about the arrests of a ring of terrorists operating in New Jersey. Repairs were made to the World Trade Center, and new safety regulations were implemented, which would be of use eight years later.

Two days after the bombing, another violent attack captured headlines across the nation. In Waco, TX, the Bureau of Alcohol,

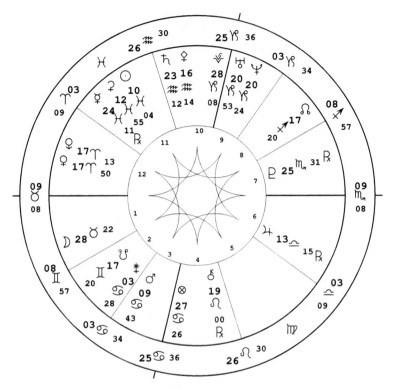

Waco Attack
February 28, 1993   9:45am CST
Waco, Texas
Koch 31N32'57" 97W08'47"

Tobacco, and Firearms attempted a raid on the compound of cult leader David Koresh. There had been reports that Koresh had been stockpiling weapons and ammunition. Former cult members told stories of abuse of children, which sparked a series of newspaper articles. The Bureau had been planning the Waco raid since 1992, and the increased publicity expedited the planning. In the chart for the Waco attack, Eris is still conjunct Venus, trine Chiron and the North Node, sextile the South Node and Pallas, and squaring the Uranus-Neptune conjunction. With Eris in the Twelfth House, it was intended to be a surprise raid, but the element of surprise was compromised by obvious Federal and media presence in the area. The Koresh followers were tipped off, and when the officers raided the compound they were met with a barrage of gunfire.

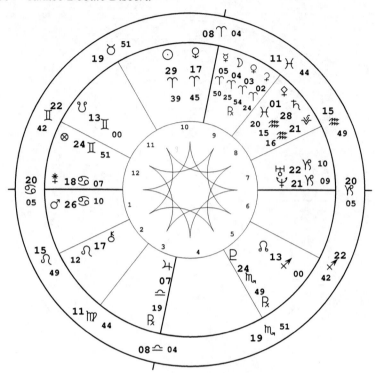

Waco Burning
April 19, 1993   12:07pm CDT
Waco, Texas
Koch 31N32'57"   97W08'47"

Four agents were killed in the raid and sixteen were wounded. Five cult members were killed in the attack. The story was so sensational, a film company started producing a TV movie of the event within weeks of the raid.

After the attack, the Koresh compound was surrounded by FBI agents. Rather than listen to counselors who dealt with cult members, the FBI applied harsh tactics by broadcasting loud rock music, dial-tones, and even Buddhist chants to upset and destabilize the people inside the compound with sleep deprivation. Negotiators agreed to Koresh's demands that a message from him be played on Christian radio. Eleven people and nineteen children did leave the compound, but a core group remained devoted to Koresh. Religious counselors warned the FBI that these people might be willing to commit mass suicide with Koresh.

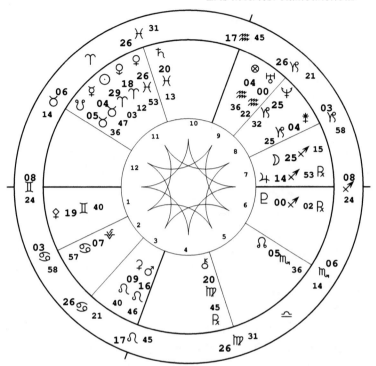

Oklahoma City Bombing
April 19, 1995   9:02 am CDT
Oklahoma City, OK
Koch 35N28'03" 97W30'58"

Finally, on April 19, 1993, the FBI started a more aggressive attack on the compound after more reports came of child abuse. A tank was sent in to punch holes in the building and release tear gas. Shortly after 12:00 pm, a fire was started in the compound by the Koresh followers, and quickly spread to all of the buildings. No fire rescue equipment was nearby and the people outside could only watch as everyone was immolated. In the chart of the burning, Eris is still trine Chiron, sextile Vesta and square Juno and Neptune. Images of the burning compound were sent around the world and created a backlash of resentment against the FBI and the Federal government.

Following the deaths in Waco, militant anti-government groups began spreading more hate propaganda against Federal authorities. This material attracted the attention of a veteran named

Timothy McVeigh, who was inspired to strike against what he saw was a dictatorship. After purchasing a ton of ammonium-nitrate fertilizer and scouting target locations, McVeigh decided to blow up the Alfred P. Murrah building in Oklahoma City. He parked a rental truck filled with the explosive fertilizer beside the building, lit the fuse, and drove away from the city in a car without a license plate.

In the chart for the explosion, Eris is trine Mars and Jupiter (forming a Grand Trine in Fire), sextile Pallas, and quincunx Chiron. The disaster would arouse world-wide sympathy for the tragic deaths of 168 people, many of them children in a day care center. The iconic image of the event would be a picture of a firefighter holding a dying infant. The FBI was able to trace the bomb truck back to McVeigh by means of a vehicle identification number on the axle. It turned out that McVeigh was already in custody, having been arrested for driving a car without a license plate. He was executed by lethal injection in 2001.

After the Oklahoma City bombing, the militia groups began toning down their anti-government rhetoric. New regulations were put into place for the construction of more security in Federal buildings. The public turned its attention to the discordian events of Princess Diana's death, Bill Clinton's sex life, and the perilous Y2K bug. Y2K inspired many to await the decline of civilization after computers worldwide would crash on New Year's Day 2000, but this became a non-event as computers and their programmers moved on into the new year without major difficulties.

Endnotes:

[1] Morris, Hugh, *The Art of Kissing*, Copyright 1936, Reprinted 1988 (pamphlet), page 28

[2] Carruth, Gordon (Editor) *The Encyclopedia of American Facts and Dates* (Seventh Edition), Thomas Y. Crowell Publishers, New York, 1979, 0-690-01669-7, page 980

Chapter 17

The Master of Camelot

Natal Discord

John F. Kennedy was born with Eris conjunct Chiron in the Sixth House (which rules health) and trine Saturn and his Midheaven. Although Kennedy appeared strong and vigorous, he did have serious health problems throughout most of his life. In 1931, he had an emergency appendectomy, which caused him to withdraw from the Canterbury Boarding School. In 1934, he was hospitalized for months with an attack of colitis. In 1936, he was under observation for two months for possible leukemia. During World War II, he injured his spine, and in the 1950's he had to undergo a series of operations to correct the spinal problems. He would be bothered by back pain for the rest of his life. There were also reports that he suffered from Addison's Disease, and some feared his health would prevent him from finishing his term in office. During his life, Kennedy received Extreme Unction (the Roman Catholic Last Rites) four times.

Eris in Aries

When Eris was trine his Neptune and sextile his Part of Fortune, Kennedy started attending high class boarding schools. Having to live in the shadow of his older brother, Joe, John became something of a hellion, performing practical jokes. While attending the Choate School, Kennedy's most notorious prank was to blow up a toilet seat with firecrackers. The head of the school held up the broken toilet seat before the student body and denounced "the muckers who spit in our sea." Kennedy took that as a compliment and formed his own "Muckers Club." Years later, he would still be friends with some of these prep school comrades.

In 1935, with Eris square his Pluto, Kennedy would take his first trip abroad with his family, and he was going to study with Professor Harold Laski at the Laski School of Economics. To this day there is a mystery concerning his stay there, which was very short. In October 1935, he enrolled at Princeton University, but only lasted six weeks before he had to be put under observation for leukemia. In 1936, he would enter Harvard, again following behind his brother, Joe.

Kennedy finally surpassed Joe in World War II, showing his courage with the sinking of PT-109. Kennedy would always say he never felt like a hero because, "it was inadvertent. They sank my boat." Brother Joe would die in an airplane explosion, leaving John F. Kennedy as his father's main hope for a political dynasty.

Kennedy served in Congress while Eris was sextile his Sun. He developed a reputation as a playboy, and became notorious for his affairs. Even after his marriage to Jackie Bouvier and his election to the Senate, he still was infamous for playing around. In a more genteel age, the press was aware of Kennedy's private actions, but would not reveal them to the public until a decade after his death.

Elected President in 1960, Kennedy was off to a difficult start by authorizing the ill-fated Bay of Pigs operation. He managed to improve his reputation by showing restraint during the Cuban missile crisis. He gained prestige by hammering the

John F. Kennedy
May 29, 1917
3:16 pm EST
Brookline, MA
Koch 42N19'54"
71W07'18"

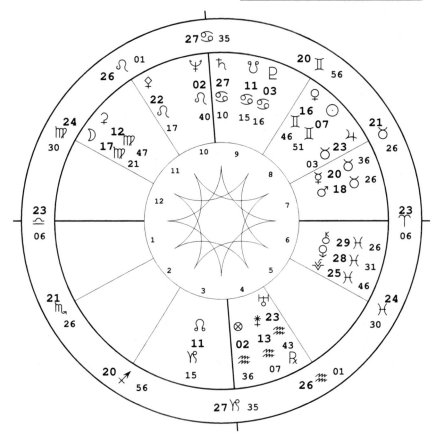

steel companies when they went back on their word and raised steel prices. He was looking forward to re-election at the time of his assassination on Nov. 22, 1963.

At the time of the assassination, Eris was conjunct Jupiter sextile the Moon, quincunx Juno and Uranus, and squaring the North and South Nodes. Juno and Uranus, sextile each other, formed a Yod aspect with Eris-Jupiter. It was a crime of the highest magnitude. With Eris trine Mercury and Vesta, the emotional shock of the event spread around the world immediately. All those alive at the time would remember where they were when they heard the news about the shooting.

After his death, Kennedy underwent his own apotheosis as numerous pictures and icons were produced commemorating his administration. Jackie Kennedy would offer up the perfect metaphor when she described the Kennedy years as being like "Camelot." The circumstances of Kennedy's death would raise issues for years as to whether he was the victim of a secret government conspiracy. Because of the enormity of the crime, many people did not want to believe that a wimpy lone gunman could be responsible for such a killing. There were plenty of other suspects to choose from: Communists, the CIA, Cuban exiles, the Mafia, and even Texas oil millionaires. It would be a time of paranoia and uncertainty as people worried about secret groups controlling the government.

In 1964, when Eris was squaring Kennedy's Nodes, the Warren Commission report was released, proclaiming that Kennedy had been killed by a lone gunman. The report was greeted with resounding skepticism. In the late 1960's, conspiracy theorists such as Jim Garrison, kept making headlines with unsubstantiated accounts of a CIA plot against Kennedy. At this time, Eris was quincunx Kennedy's Ceres, and as the Nixon administration came to power and the Vietnam War was escalated, the publicity helped remind the public of how much of a considerate leader the nation had lost when Kennedy died.

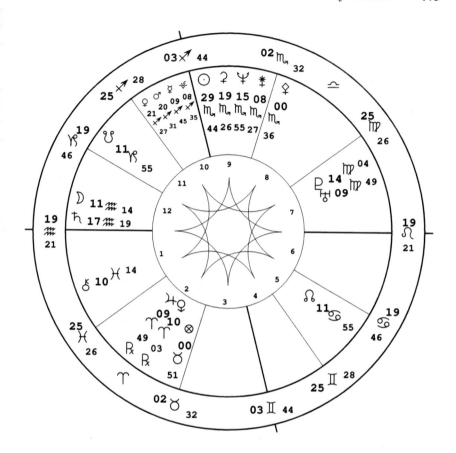

JFK Assassination
November 22, 1963
12:30 pm CST
Dallas, Texas
Koch 32N47 96W48

Chapter 18
Prince von Metternich
goes to Washington

Heinz Alfred Kissinger was born in Furth, Germany, the son of a schoolteacher. In 1938, Eris was sextile his Sun when the Nazi persecution of Jews escalated, and the Kissinger family sought safety by moving to New York. Though Heinz became Henry and fit in well with American society, he still retained his foreign accent. He attended night school and worked in a shaving brush factory during the day. After getting a high school diploma, he studied accounting at the City College of New York until he was drafted into the army in 1943.

When Kissinger was assigned to the 84th Infantry Division, he met another fellow German émigré, Fritz Kraemer, who appreciated Kissinger's brains and had him assigned to military intelligence. Kissinger saw action at the Battle of the Bulge and volunteered for hazardous intelligence duties. After the war, he used his knowledge of German society to help with the "denazification" program in setting up civilian governments in German cities.

In 1950, Eris was sextile Kissinger's Mercury, and he received a B.A. degree (summa cum laude) from Harvard. It was

Henry Kissinger

Prince von Metternich

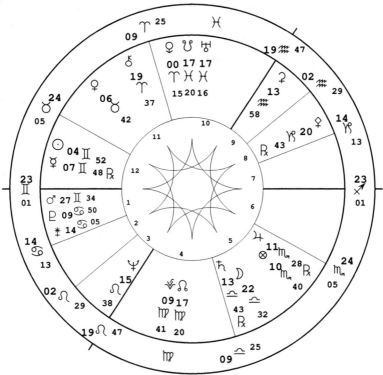

Henry Kissinger
May 27, 1923
5:30 am CET
Furth, Germany
Koch 49N29 10E59

also under this transit that he married Ann Fleischer. The marriage produced a son and a daughter, and ended in divorce in 1964. Kissinger was moving higher in the world of academia, and he would earn an M.A. and a Ph.D. His doctoral dissertation was a study on the statesmanship of Castlereagh and Metternich.

Klemens Wenzel, Prince von Metternich was a personal hero of Kissinger. Metternich was seen as the creator of "realpolitik", which was politics based on practical considerations and not ideology. After the fall of Napoleon, Metternich was the leader of foreign policy in Europe, and for thirty years helped to maintain a peaceful balance of power between nations, to the benefit of the Austro-Hungarian Empire. Though some saw him as reactionary, he maintained a reputation as a clever diplomat who was a master of political calculation.

Kissinger entered the world of "realpolitik" when Eris entered his Eleventh House, squaring his Pluto, and quincunx his Vesta. His skills brought him within the fold of the Rockefeller family, working for the Special Studies Project of the Rockefeller Brothers Fund. He became an advisor to Nelson Rockefeller, governor of New York, who made three unsuccessful bids for the GOP presidential nomination. It was this association that helped Kissinger make contacts with figures in Republican Party politics.

During the 1960's, when Eris was quincunx his Part of Fortune, Kissinger was building his reputation by working as Director of the Harvard International Seminar, and as a consultant to the Operations Research Office, the State Department, and the Rand Corporation. He also attracted attention because of his ideas supporting using nuclear weapons to fight a "limited nuclear war." One rumor circulating was that Kissinger was really the model for "Dr. Strangelove", which was denied by Stanley Kubrick and Peter Sellers.

In 1969, with Eris quincunx his Jupiter, Kissinger was brought into the Nixon administration as National Security Advisor. He started applying "realpolitik" to an administration that had been noted for its anti-communist ideology. Rather than get tough with the Russians, Kissinger advocated a "détente" to ease tensions in the Cold War. To make the Russians more agreeable for negotiation, Kissinger began secret talks with the government of the People's Republic of China. This brought about a thawing of the relations between America and China, allowing the American ping-pong team to compete in China. In 1954, Secretary of State John Foster Dulles refused to shake hands with Chinese Premier Zhou Enlai. Vice-President Richard Nixon praised Dulles for not being deceived by the Chinese. Eighteen years later, Nixon would abandon his "red scare" ideology and embrace the "realpolitik" of recognizing the People's Republic of China. Through Kissinger's diplomacy, Nixon would shake hands with Zhou Enlai and Chairman Mao Zedong. The possibility of an American/Chinese alliance pressured the Russians into signing the Strategic Arms Limitation Treaty, making the old-time Cold Warrior Nixon look like a peace-seeking President.

The Presidency of Richard Nixon was still under the shadow of the Vietnam War, which had been escalated and brought attacks on Laos and Cambodia. Kissinger took over the negotiations of the Paris Peace Talks, and before the 1972 election was able to announce that, "Peace is at hand." America's role in the war would end in 1973 with the return of troops. Kissinger received the 1973 Nobel Peace Prize, which he accepted with what he called "humility."

In 1973, with Eris opposing his Saturn, Kissinger was made Secretary of State, officially being given credit for the foreign policy successes of the past four years. He established a reputation as a world-traveler for the cause of peace. His most successful effort would bring about an end to the Yom Kippur war between Israel and Egypt by means of his "shuttle diplomacy". His talents made him the most popular figure in the Nixon Administration, and he remained untarnished when the rest of the Nixon White House faced investigation during the Watergate scandal.

At the same time, Eris was also sextile his Ceres, and not all of his activities were completely benign. As a ruthless part of his "realpolitik", Kissinger supported the coup in Chile, which brought in a military junta that ruled the country with an iron hand. He justified it as necessary to prevent another Communist regime from establishing itself in the hemisphere. The stories of human right abuses would play havoc with Kissinger's image as a peacemaker.

Kissinger had often presented a public image of himself as a playboy, appearing at parties with various Hollywood sex symbols. In 1974, with Eris squaring his Juno, he surprised everyone by marrying Nancy Maginnes, who worked for him as a researcher. The previous year she had denied rumors that they were romantically involved. They seemed to make an unusual couple, since Nancy was several inches taller than Kissinger, giving the pair a Mutt-and-Jeff appearance.

After the resignation of Richard Nixon, Kissinger stayed on as Secretary of State in the Ford administration. He would see his work at the Paris Peace Talks undone when North Vietnam overwhelmed South Vietnam, causing an embarrassing evacuation of American personnel. The American public wanted nothing more to do with the Vietnam War and would not support any effort to aid South Vietnam.

With the defeat of Gerald Ford in 1976, Kissinger left government service and returned to his role as a consultant. With Eris trine his Neptune, he began working with numerous foreign policy organizations, including the Trilateral Commission, which became the target of many conspiracy theorists who suggested it was a front for world government. He would form Kissinger Associates, which was his own consulting firm for advising clients on worldwide government relations. Somehow, he managed to find time to even become chairman of the North American Soccer League.

By the 1990's, with Eris quincunx his North Node, Kissinger was regarded as an elder statesman, still avidly sought out for political advice behind the scenes (a role once played by Metternich.) He was invited to meetings of the Bilderbergers, another group suspected of one-world government by conspiracy theorists. Kissinger rarely gave interviews, leaving some to question his motives in getting involved in secret activities.

In 1998, with Eris conjunct his Chiron, Kissinger mourned the passing of his elderly mother. Under the same transit, he entered into a partnership with Mack McLarty, who was President

Bill Clinton's childhood friend and chief-of-staff. With Eris square Kissinger's Pallas, they provided consultations to the administration of George W. Bush. Kissinger supported the Iraq war, but complained that too few troops had been used and that the Iraqi army should not have been disbanded. The partnership with McLarty ended in January, 2008.

As of this writing, Kissinger has Eris in opposition to his Moon, and it may be a time for him to concentrate on his legacy and what sort of memorial he wants to leave behind. Some have suggested he should be put on trial for war crimes for his involvements that destabilized the governments of Cambodia and Chile. Others have questioned his associations with corporations and political organizations. Like his role model, Metternich, he has come to be seen as a reactionary thwarting the will of the people. Perhaps Kissinger's legacy can be summed up by one of his most famous quotes: "Power is the ultimate aphrodisiac."

Chapter 19
The Great Communicator

Natal Discord

Ronald Reagan was born with Eris in the Third House squaring Pluto and sextile Uranus. During his career he became famous for his quips and one-line comments which would be best used for TV news clips. Phrases like, "There you go again," "Honey, I forgot to duck," and "Mr. Gorbachev, tear down this wall" were markers for his career as a communicator. However, in later years, some questioned how much substance there was behind the sound bites.

As the young Ronald Reagan was growing up, his family was on the move, living above storefronts and never settling into a stable home. Eris was square Reagan's Ascendant at this time. Reagan's family would impress upon him the goodness of people, and he would use that positive attitude in his personal expression towards others. The Reagan family rejected the racial prejudice prevalent at the time. Reagan recalled that in Dixon, IL, when the local hotels rejected black guests, the Reagan family would offer them food and shelter.

Ronald Reagan
February 6, 1911
4:16 am CST
Tampico, Illinois
Koch   41N37'49"
80W47'10"

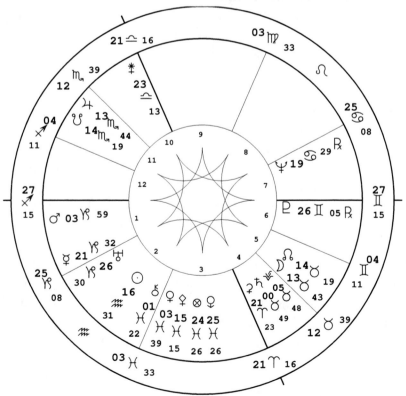

Eris in Aries

Reagan was blessed with handsome features and a muscular build, which helped him as he grew older and worked as a lifeguard, excelled at football in college, and later became a radio sports announcer. In 1937, with Eris squaring his Mars, Reagan's macho good looks paid off with a Hollywood screen test, and a contract with Warner Brothers studios. Though he appeared in a number of B pictures, he also attracted attention in supporting roles in films like "Santa Fe Trail" and "King's Row." Even when he had to stand in the shadow of stars like Errol Flynn and Bette Davis, he was still able to make his screen presence known.

Reagan later became head of the Screen Actor's Guild, had an unsuccessful marriage to Jane Wyman, and then helped lead the fight in Hollywood against Communist infiltration. Originally a New Deal Democrat, Reagan changed his political affiliation after he married Nancy Davis in the 1950's. While still appearing in movies, he embraced the new medium of television, and made numerous appearances on shows and commercials, notably "GE Theater" and "Death Valley Days."

In the 1960's, Reagan's support for Republican candidates made GOP leaders in California see him as a possible governor. Elected in 1966, and serving until 1975, he became a national figure for the Republican Party. After the scandals of Watergate, the Republicans began searching for "outsiders" who were not tainted by the corruption in Washington, D.C. With Eris quincunx his Jupiter, Reagan began moving towards the Presidency. He narrowly lost the nomination in 1976, but was able to easily capture it in 1980, when Eris was quincunx his South Node.

After winning by a landslide, Reagan was inaugurated as President, but then nearly lost his life in an assassination attempt by a crazed lone gunman. (See the chart on the next page.) In the chart of the shooting, Eris was in the Eighth House, along with Mars, the Sun, and Venus. Eris was sextile the Part of Fortune, and Reagan believed he was blessed by God to survive such an attack so that he could go on to fulfill a greater purpose. Reagan's recovery was considered miraculous because he had been shot in the lung with a "Devastator" bullet, which failed to explode, and he had lost

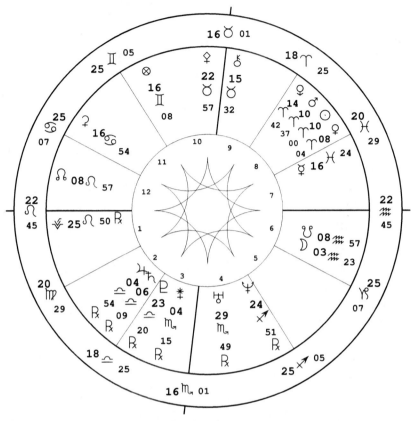

Reagan Shooting
March 30, 1981, 2:30 pm EST
Washington, D.C.
Koch 38N53'42" 77W02'12"

half his blood volume. With Eris square Ceres, he got widespread sympathy and support during his recovery. On the operating table, he asked his doctors if they were Republicans. The doctors assured him they were, if only in spirit to save his life.

Reagan's jaunty humor in the face of adversity increased his popularity. People enjoyed listening to his stories and anecdotes, not caring that he got his names and dates mixed up, or that he was referring to non-existent people. When reporters questioned the White House Press Secretary Larry Speakes about these erroneous stories, his response was, "If you tell the same story five times, it's true." [1]

Reagan was re-elected by a landslide in 1984, and there were hopes for another four years of good feelings and nice stories. However, as Eris was sextile Reagan's Sun, there were events that were to make people question his hold on power. In 1985, Reagan underwent surgery for cancerous polyps in his colon. The surgery was successful and Reagan was able to return to work. Then the Reagan administration was shaken by the Iran-Contra scandal, and his legacy was tarnished by the admission that he was not in complete control of events in the government.

Colonel Oliver North, operating in the basement of the White House, had conducted a clandestine program in selling arms to Iran, which was fighting a war with Iraq. Colonel North took the profits from those arms sales, and diverted them to the Contras in Nicaragua, even though Congress had passed the Boland Amendment, banning all aid to the Contras because of their violations of human rights. The plot was exposed by a Lebanese magazine in November, 1986, and confirmed when an arms shipment from the US to the Contras was intercepted by the Nicaraguan government.

Colonel North and his minions took the blame for the scandal, but the revelations would tarnish Reagan's administration. Investigations by Congress and the Tower Commission showed that Reagan was not aware of what was happening with his National Security Council. Reagan would publicly take the blame for his lack of attention. It caused a dramatic drop in his popularity. Further attacks on Reagan would come from his former chief of staff, Donald Regan, who complained that the Reagans listened to an astrologer more than they listened to him.

Reagan was able to leave office with his popularity intact, but after a while people began asking questions about how well mentally connected he was as a leader. In 1994, Reagan publicly admitted that he was diagnosed with Alzheimer's, and questions arose as to whether the memory loss was manifesting during the White House years. The Reagans withdrew from public appearances. His finale was marked with a touching public letter, asking for privacy so that he and his family could deal with his condition.

In 2001, as Reagan approached his 90th birthday with Eris square Neptune, he slipped and broke his hip. The damage was repaired at once, but Reagan faced a difficult period of physical therapy. In 2004, as Eris was approaching a sextile to his Mercury, an opposition to his Midheaven, and a conjunction to his Ceres, Ronald Reagan passed away and was given a huge funeral. Lying in state in both the Ronald Reagan Library and the US Capitol, his body was viewed by more than 100,000 people in each location.

Shortly before the Washington D.C. funeral took place there was a false terrorist alert, when the Governor of Kentucky, flying to the funeral in a private plane, veered off his flight path and was assumed to be another flying terrorist about to crash his plane into the Capitol. There was a temporary evacuation of the Capitol, but after the error was discovered, the funeral went ahead as planned.

Endnote:

[1] Slansky, Paul, *The Clothes Have No Emperor,* Fireside Books-Simon & Schuster, New York, 1989, 0-671-67339-4, page 79.

Chapter 20

Eris in the 21st Century
Wounding the Healer

In the Summer of 2001, Eris was opposing the USA Juno, conjunct the USA Chiron, and sextile the USA Part of Fortune. It was a time of political wrangling and business as usual. Then, on the day of infamy, Sept. 11, transiting Eris in the Seventh House (house of marriage, but also enemies) was sextile Uranus, trine Venus and Chiron, and quincunx the Sun. At 8:46 am, an airliner collided with the North Tower of the World Trade Center. With Mercury on the Ascendant, news of the collision spread far and wide, with TV images from traffic helicopters showing the burning wreckage.

For several minutes, it was hoped that this was just an isolated incident, a terrible aviation error. Then, at 9:03 am, as Eris was opposing the Ascendant and squaring the Midheaven, a second airliner crashed into the South Tower of the World Trade Center. From that moment on, there was no doubt it was a terrorist attack, and further reports would come in about an airliner crashing into the Pentagon and a fourth airliner crashing in the fields of Pennsylvania.

It was a time of horror, but it was also a time of courage and sympathy. New York City firemen suffered losses as they

**Attack
on the World
Trade Center**
September 11, 2001
8:46 am EDT
New York, NY
Koch 40N42'51"
74W00'23"

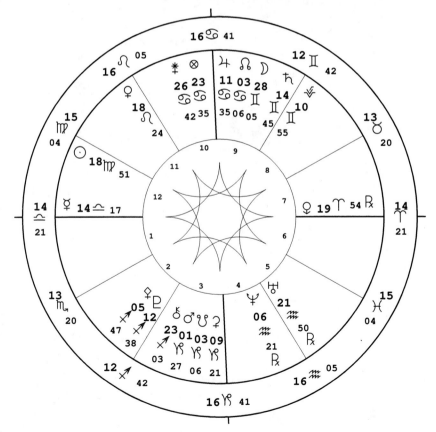

evacuated the twin towers and fire crews would be killed by the collapse. Pentagon workers would flee their burning building, but then turn around to volunteer to help those trapped inside. Messages of sympathy came in from around the world, even from nations that had bitter feelings towards the USA. It was a world-wide outpouring of condolences rarely seen in recent history.

Yet, after the dust had settled, a period of discord began. Sympathy would give away to xenophobia, as some people blamed all Muslims for the terrorist attack. The draconian Patriot Act

was passed to give extra governmental powers in tracking down terrorists. Overnight, political dissent was muted. The public was bombarded with fearful stories of anthrax killers, shoe bombers, and weapons of mass destruction. Leaders were able to stir up war fever based on spurious evidence.

A Heck of a Job

In August, 2005, a national disaster took place that would take the public's minds off of foreign wars. Hurricane Katrina was approaching the Gulf of Mexico coast with 125 mph winds. The governor of Louisiana and the mayor of New Orleans ordered an evacuation of people living in the low-lying areas. Unfortunately, thousands of poor people who did not own cars were trapped as

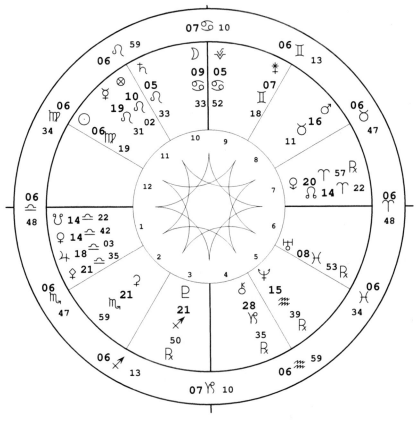

Hurricane Katrina
August 29, 2005
9:00 am CDT
New Orleans, LA
Koch 20N57'16" 90W04'30"

the storm hit. At 9:00 am on August 29, the levees around New Orleans started to burst, devastating the city with a horrific flood.

The chart for the flood shows Eris trine Pluto and Mercury, causing a Grand Trine in Fire. The destruction and death toll were the result of miscommunication and poor organizational planning. With Eris opposing Jupiter and Pallas, private relief organizations began collecting funds and sending supplies to New Orleans. Eris quincunx Ceres marked an outpouring of sympathy and generosity from the rest of the nation.

Television images showed people trapped on rooftops, waving

to helicopters to carry them away. Reports came in about refugees taking shelter in the Super Dome, which was not designed for providing shelter against a hurricane. There were not enough sanitary facilities in the giant stadium, causing hygienic problems until supplies could be air-lifted in. Thousands of people leaving the city were sent to refugee centers in Texas.

With more than 1500 dead in the disaster, finger-pointing began with Federal and Louisiana officials criticizing each other. Most of the criticism was aimed at Michael Brown, the head of the Federal Emergency Management Agency (FEMA). Formerly in charge of an Arabian horse association, Brown received his appointment to FEMA because he was friends with the Bush campaign manager. Brown criticized Louisiana officials for not acting fast enough to prepare for the storm. Louisiana officials complained about Brown's lack of preparedness and the delay in getting supplies to the Gulf coast. President Bush tried to improve Brown's professional appearance by publicly making the remark, "Brownie, you're doing a heck of a job." Yet, Brown ended up resigning from FEMA, and his reputation for incompetence was finally demonstrated by the release of flippant e-mails written during the Katrina disaster which proved his focus was not on the serious nature of the event.

For nearly eight years, Eris stayed near the 2001 positions in the USA chart, bringing upheaval to each area. With Eris sextile the USA Part of Fortune, the fortunes of the elite were increased with tax cuts, deregulation, and discordant schemes. Banks and lending houses were discovered to be filled with toxic investments instead of capital. By 2008, it was found that "respectable" brokers were really running a Ponzi scheme of seeking new investors to pay off the old investors.

With Eris conjunct USA Chiron, the issue of healing was a major topic of discussion, as it became apparent that the health care system was not functioning properly. Citizens were in a nightmare situation of being caught between Kafkaesque insurance regulations and ever-increasing medical costs. Medical expenses were starting to force people into bankruptcy, and the public began pushing for a solution.

Eris in opposition to USA Juno brought out interesting debates on the nature of marriage. Arguments for gay marriage have been presented for several years, with opponents claiming that marriage is between a man and a woman, and its purpose is to produce children. The courts and state legislatures have been hearing arguments on gay marriage, and concluded that gays have been discriminated against because of the marriage laws. With the opposition to Juno, gays could end up with marriage rights, which could be a financial boost to the wedding industry.

At this writing, Eris is now sextile the USA Mars, and the administration of President Barack Obama has inherited the wars of the previous administration. With this sextile, it may prove to be difficult to get out of the quagmire situations of these wars. The sextile will continue until 2013, suggesting that the Obama administration will be plagued by wars it did not start and did not want to keep going. Difficulty in managing the wars will definitely be a political issue as the 2012 election comes up.

There may also be rumblings, grumblings, and threats of civil war as a militant spirit spreads across the land, but as with Eris trine USA Mars in the 1830's, these threats will not manifest into a full-scale rebellion. However, the anti-government hatred may be sowing the seeds for future conflict, as John C. Calhoun and other secessionists did, which inspired secession in the 1860's.

With Eris in the Sixth house of the USA chart, the health care debate will be a continued struggle. There has been increased hostility over the role of government in private matters. Some citizens claim they are ready to take up arms rather than have government health care. Others complain about a sell-out because the new plan does not provide enough coverage. Even with the health care package passed, there will be people constantly complaining about it while Eris is conjunct the USA Chiron.

Finally, another current Eris aspect is a quincunx to the USA Neptune. The major news story as this book is going to print is about the British Petroleum oil spill in the Gulf of Mexico. There has been havoc with oil and tar balls washing up on the beaches, and wildlife being contaminated. Although BP has been taking a lot of public relations heat, and they will have to pay out reparations, the oil industry may not suffer from this accident in the long run. There will be talk of alternative energy sources, but the oil producers are too much a part of the industrial infrastructure to be easily replaced. It is possible the oil companies could use the spill to refute the claims of conservationists that the world is running out of oil, by pointing out that there is plenty of oil in the Gulf of Mexico, though it needs to be handled carefully.

The last time Eris was quincunx USA Neptune was in the 1830s when the Whig party was created. The Whigs were a crazy quilt of political factions, united by a common thread of hatred for Andrew Jackson and his politics, which were seen as giving too much power to the Federal government. The original Whigs were British politicians in the 18th century who opposed too much influence by the King, and were in favor of a limited monarchy. The American Whigs referred to Jackson as "King Andrew" and supported a limit to Federal control. The current Eris quincunx USA Neptune transit has marked the rise of the Tea Party. Like the Whigs, factions that want to limit the power of the Federal government make up the Tea Party, and a common thread of attacking Barack Obama unites them. So far they have not come up with a spokesperson as eloquent as Henry Clay. Any political victories by the Tea Party may be limited, and after a while they are likely to break down in the manner of the Whig Party.

Chapter 21
Eris into the future:
Watch Uranus!

Where does Eris go from here? From 2018 to 2025, Eris will be square the USA Mercury. This may mark a time when the mass media will be reduced to electronic blips. Anyone with a cell phone camera and a Facebook or MySpace listing will be a potential journalist. This may raise questions about journalistic ethics, especially if each citizen is given a chance to have a microphone. It may take freedom of the press issues to a new level, with blogs replacing editorial pages and internet radio replacing broadcasters. The downside is that it may see the proliferation of scurrilous stories of the sort that plagued poor John Adams. Censorship and editorial control may not be possible in a world of numerous wireless servers and a myriad of internet addresses. Also, issues of privacy may be at risk, if cameras are everywhere.

In 2026, the 250th anniversary of the United States will see Eris sextile the USA Moon. Instead of a time of pleasant nostalgia, this may be a time of emotional discord, with different factions wrangling over who is most fit to represent "America." The arguments may continue on into 2027, in time for the USA

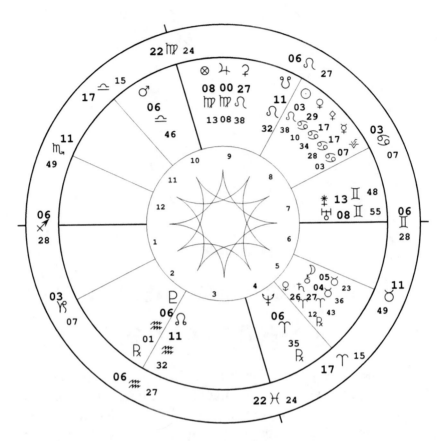

2027 Uranus Return
July 26, 2027
4:23 pm EDT
Washington D.C.
Koch 38N53'42" 77W02'12"

Uranus return. These 84-year events have previously marked periods of intense warfare and change in the nation. In 1860, the Uranus return was when South Carolina seceded from the Union. In 1944, the second Uranus return was at the end of May, when final preparations were being made for the D-Day invasion, on which hung the course of World War II.

With Eris sextile the USA Moon, the third Uranus return could see another period of warfare, with a possible rebellion taking place against the central government. With the sentiments raised by the 250th anniversary of Independence, people might decide, "If our ancestors could do it, then why can't we?" Divided anti-government factions may find common cause under a new leader, and there would be a fervor to fight in the spirit of 1776.

July 26, 2027 is the date of the next USA Uranus return, and it is marked with a Grand Trine in Air with Uranus, Mars, and Pluto. At this time, it might mainly be a war of words, with violent verbiage filling the airwaves. Eris will be conjunct Saturn, and it is possible conservative figures will be leading the discord. Eris will also be trine Ceres in Leo, suggesting that the farming community will be involved with the conflict as well. With Eris and Saturn squaring Venus, there may be some attempts at peacemaking, but with Venus void-of-course they may prove to be futile.

From the sextile with the USA Moon, Eris will pass to a sextile with the USA Pallas. The discordian sextiles will last from 2025 to 2032, and during these years of struggle there may be a wasting of talents, a lack of development and growth, and a polarizing of social and political views. The struggle may not be so much a battle of state versus state as much as it would be faction versus faction. The issues of the factions could be unimaginable by today's standards. History has shown that the Union was nearly broken up by unpopular warfare, an embargo, the tariff, and slavery. As today we can not imagine an embargo causing civil unrest, we may not understand the causes of future unrest.

In 2032, Eris will be square the USA Pluto, and that could bring about the necessary change in government (rather than its abolishment) to end the conflict. The times could see a new President willing to offer amnesty to the warring factions. As Eris moves back and forth with the sextile to Pallas and the square to Pluto, it may be a slow process of healing. Some factions will have to force others into accepting the peace. The result may be a different nation with different values by the time that Eris moves into Taurus in 2050.

At this point, it would be appropriate to conclude with a quote from Daniel Webster:

I have not allowed myself, sir, to look beyond the Union, to see what might be hidden in the dark recess behind. I have not coolly weighed the chances of preserving liberty when the bonds that unite us together shall be broken asunder. I have not accustomed myself to hang over the precipice of disunion, to see whether, with my short sight, I can fathom the depth of the abyss below; nor could I regard him as a safe counselor in the affairs in this government whose thoughts should be mainly bent on considering, not how the Union may be best preserved but how tolerable might be the condition of the people when it should be broken up and destroyed. While the Union lasts, we have high, exciting, gratifying prospects spread out before us, for us and our children. Beyond that I seek not to penetrate the veil.

God grant that in my day, at least, that curtain may not rise! God grant that on my vision never may be opened what lies behind! When my eyes shall be turned to behold for the last time the sun in heaven, may I not see him shining on the broken and dishonored fragments of a once glorious Union; on states dissevered, discordant, belligerent; on a land rent with civil feuds, or drenched, it may be, in fraternal blood! Let their last feeble and lingering glance rather behold the gorgeous ensign of the republic, now known and honored throughout the earth, still full high advanced, its arms and trophies streaming in their original luster, not a stripe erased or polluted, nor a single star obscured, bearing for its motto, no such miserable interrogatory as "What is all this worth?" nor those other words of delusion and folly, "Liberty first and Union afterwards"; but everywhere, spread all over in characters of living light, blazing on all its ample folds, as they float over the sea and over the land, and in every wind under the whole heavens, that other sentiment, dear to every true American heart-Liberty and Union, now and forever, one and inseparable!

Bibliography

Birth Data from AstroDataBank   **Rodden Rating**

King George III . . . . A
Benjamin Franklin . . . . DD
George Washington . . . . AA
Martha Washington C
John Hancock . . . . DD
Thomas Jefferson . . . . DD
John Adams C
Andrew Jackson . . . . DD
Abraham Lincoln . . . . B
Theodore Roosevelt . . . . B
Franklin Delano Roosevelt . . . . AA
J. Edgar Hoover XX
John F. Kennedy . . . . A
Henry Kissinger . . . . AA
Ronald Reagan . . . . DD

Birth Data from Internet Sources

All web links cited were functioning as of June 26, 2010.

Data and information about the discovery of Planet Eris
  http://www.gps.caltech.edu/~mbrown/planetlila/
Wolfstar's Scorpio Rising Chart for the USA
  http://www.neptunecafe.com/Main.html

Alexander Hamilton Death
  *http://colonial-america.suite101.com/article.cfm/the-
  hamilton-burr-duel---details-and-results*

The Star Spangled Banner
  http://www.infoplease.com/ipa/A0194015.html

Fort Sumter   *http://www.us-civilwar.com/sumter.htm*

Gettysburg   *http://www.visit-gettysburg.com/the-battle-of-
  gettysburg-timeline.html*

Lincoln Assassination *http://www.u-s-history.com/pages/h124.html*
Wounded Knee *http://www.dreamscape.com/morgana/wknee.htm*
Dow Jones Worst Day
    *http://www.cnbc.com/id/27119471/Dow_and_the_
    Depression*
Pearl Harbor
    *http://en.wikipedia.org/wiki/Attack_on_Pearl_
    Harbor#CITEREFPrange1999*
    Citation: *Prange, Gordon W. (1999), Goldstein, ed.,
    The Pearl Harbor Papers: Inside the Japanese Plans,
    Brassey's, ISBN 1574882228*
Franklin Roosevelt Death
    *http://docs.fdrlibrary.marist.edu/PSF/BOX20/T901AY01.
    HTML*
Hiroshima
    http://www.cfo.doe.gov/me70/manhattan/hiroshima.htm
JFK Assassination
    *http://www.jfklibrary.org/Historical+Resources/
    JFK+in+History/Death+of+the+President.htm*
Civil Rights Act 1964
    *http://www.archives.gov/education/lessons/civil-rights-
    act/images/act-08.jpg*
Martin Luther King Jr. Assassination
    *http://www.time.com/time/specials/2007
    article/0,28804,1726656_1726689,00.html*
Robert Kennedy Assassination *http://www.robertfkennedy.net/*
Nixon Resignation
    http://www.historyplace.com/speeches/nixon.htm
Reagan Shooting
    *http://www.doctorzebra.com/prez/z_x40shooting_
    chronology_g.htm*
1993 World *Trade Center Bombing*
    http://www.fdnewyork.com/wtc.asp
Waco Attack   *http://uk.ask.com/wiki/Waco_Siege*

Waco Fire

> *http://www.usmessageboard.com/law-and-justice-*
> *system/106446-moon-occult-venus-in-aries-19-april-*
> *1993-the-astrology-of-the-waco-fire.html*

Oklahoma City Bombing

> *http://www.oklahomacitybombing.com/oklahoma-city-*
> *bombing.html*

September 11, 2001

> *http://www.astro.com/astro-databank/Terrorist:_*
> *WTC_%282001%29*

Hurricane K*atrina*

> *http://www.brookings.edu/fp/projects/homeland/*
> *katrinatimeline.pdf*

Internet Sources for Other Information

The Mythology of Eris

> *http://www.theoi.com/Daimon/Eris.html*

The World Turned Upside Down

> *http://www.contemplator.com/england/worldtur.html*

Broadway Musical "1776"   *http://1776themusical.us/*

Daniel Webster's Liberty & Union speech

> *http://www.usa-patriotism.com/speeches/dwebster1.htm*

George Washington *http://www.cato.org/pub_display.php?pub_id=5593*

Martha Washington *http://MarthaWashington.us*

Benedict Arnold   *http://www.benedictarnold.org*

John Hancock   *http://www.theamericanrevolution.org/*
> *peopledetail.aspx?people=8*

Endicott Peabody

> *http://en.wikipedia.org/wiki/Endicott_Peabody_(educator)*

Henry Kissinger

> *http://nobelprize.org/nobel_prizes/peace/laureates/1973/*
> *kissinger-bio.html*

http://en.wikipedia.org/wiki/Kissinger_Associates
http://en.wikipedia.org/wiki/Metternich
http://en.wikipedia.org/wiki/Realpolitik

Book Sources
** Indicates source of birth data for persons whose data source was not previously cited

Allen, Thomas & Polmar, Norman, Gassing Japan, MHQ: *The Quarterly Journal of Military History*, Autumn 1997, New York, 07485164942873

Anthony, Carl Sferranza, *First Ladies: The Saga of the President's Wives and their Power 1789-1961*, William Morrow & Co. Inc, New York, 1990, 0-688-11272-2

Augur, Helen, "Benjamin Franklin and the French Alliance," *American Heritage: The Magazine of History, Vol. VII, Number 3*, New York, April, 1956

**Bobbe, Dorothie, "The Boyhood of Alexander Hamilton," *American Heritage: The Magazine of History, Vol. VI, Number 4*, New York, June, 1955

Brodie, Fawn, "The Great Jefferson Taboo," *American Heritage: The Magazine of History, Vol. XXIII, Number 4*, New York, June, 1972,

Burstein, Andrew, *The Inner Jefferson*, University Press of Virginia, Charlottesville, VA, 1997, 0-8139-1720-4

Carruth, Gordon (Editor) *The Encyclopedia of American Facts and Dates* (Seventh Edition), Thomas Y. Crowell Publishers, New York, 1979, 0-690-01669-7

Coles, Harry L., *The War of 1812*, The University of Chicago Press, Chicago, IL, 1965, 0-226-11350-7

Commager, Henry Steel, "Jefferson and the Book Burners," *American Heritage: The Magazine of History, Vol. IX, Number 5*, New York, August, 1958

Degregorio, William A., *The Complete Book of U.S. Presidents,* Wings Books, New York, 1993, 0-517-08244-6

Doane, Doris Chase *Horoscopes of the U.S. Presidents,* Professional Astrologers Inc., Hollywood, CA 1971

Ellis, Joseph J., A*merican Sphinx: The Character of Thomas Jefferson,* Random House Inc, New York, 1998, 0-679-76441-0

Ferling, John, *Myths of the American Revolution,* Smithsonian Magazine, Vol. 40, Number 10, Washington, D.C., January, 2010

Flagel, Thomas R. *The History Buff's Guide to the Presidents,* Cumberland House, Naperville, IL, 2007, 978-1-58182-613-5

Fleming, Thomas, *1776: Year of Illusions,* W.W. Norton & Company, Inc., New York, 1975, 0-393-05542-6

Flexner, James Thomas, *Washington: The Indispensable Man,* New American Library, New York, NY, 1984, 0-462-25542-2

Garrison, Webb, *White House Ladies: Fascinating Tales and Colorful Curiosities,* Rutledge Hill Press, Nashville, TN, 1996, 1-55853-417-2

Hofstader, Richard, "The Myth of the Happy Yeoman," *American Heritage: The Magazine of History, Vol. VII, Number 3,* New York, April, 1956

Holland, Barbara, *Hail to the Chiefs: How to tell your Polks from your Tylers,* Ballantine Books, New York, 1990, 0-345-36273-x

Isaacson, Walter, *Benjamin Franklin: An American Life,* Simon & Schuster Paperbacks, New York, 2003, 978-0-7432-5807-4

Kerr, Joan Paterson, "Benjamin Franklin's Years in London," *American Heritage: The Magazine of History, Vol. XXVIII, Number 1,* New York, December, 1976

Ketchum, Richard M., "England's Vietnam: The American Revolution," *American Heritage: The Magazine of History, Vol. XXII, Number 4*, New York, June, 1971

Logan, Andy, JFK: "The Stained-Glass Image," *American Heritage: The Magazine of History, Vol. XVIII, Number 5*, New York, August, 1967

Mandel, Susan, "Hard Times: Nine Recessions That Give These Times a Little Perspective," *American History, Vol. 45, No. 1*, Leesburg, VA, April, 2010, ISSN 1076-8866

McCullough, David, *John Adams*, Simon & Schuster, New York, 2001, 0-684-81363-7

Meacham, Jon, *American Lion: Andrew Jackson in the White House*, Random House Trade Paperback, New York, 2009, 978-0-8129-7346-4

Morris, Hugh, *The Art of Kissing*, Copyright 1936, Reprinted 1988 (pamphlet)

Nettles, Curtis, *George Washington and American Independence*, Little, Brown, and Company, Boston, 1951

Nevins, Allan, "The Place of Franklin D. Roosevelt in History," *American Heritage: The Magazine of History, Vol. XVII, Number 4*, New York, June, 1966

Parton, James; Thorndike, Joseph J.; Jensen, Oliver; Ketchum, Richard; Catton, Bruce (Editors), *The American Heritage Book of the Presidents and Famous Americans, Vol. 1-12*, American Heritage Publishing Co., New York, 1967.

Persico, Joseph E., "The Great Swine Flu Epidemic of 1918," *American Heritage: The Magazine of History, Vol. XXVII, Number 4*, New York, June, 1976

Plumb, J. H., "Our Last King," *American Heritage: The Magazine of History, Vol. XI, No. 4*, New York, June 1960

Pottenger, Maritha *The Big Four Asteroids: Ceres, Pallas, Juno & Vesta*: A free information special provided by Astro Computing Service.

Pottenger, Rique, *The New American Ephemeris for the 20th Century 1900-2000 at Midnight*, Starcrafts Publishing, Exeter, NH, 2008, 9780976242291

Pottenger, Rique, *The New American Ephemeris for the 21st Century 2000-2100 at Midnight*, Starcrafts Publishing, Exeter, NH, 2006, 9780976242239

Regan, Geoffrey, Snafu: *Great American Military Disasters*, Avon Books, New York, 1993, 0-380-76755-4

Slansky, Paul, *The Clothes Have No Emperor*, Fireside Books-Simon & Schuster, New York, 1989, 0-671-67339-4

Souli, Sofia, *Greek Mythology*, Michael Toubis Publications, Attiki, Greece, 1995, 960-540-110-x

**Stone, Irving, *They Also Ran*, Pyramid Books, New York, 1964

Swindler, William F, "The Letters of Publius," *American Heritage: The Magazine of History, Vol.XII, Number 4*, New York, June, 1961

Turner, William W., *Hoover's FBI*, Dell Publishing Company, New York, 1971

**Van Doren, Carl, *Secret History of the American Revolution*, The Viking Press, New York, 1941 (birth data for Benedict Arnold).

Vaughn, Alden T., "The Horrid and Unnatural Rebellion of Daniel Shays," *American Heritage: The Magazine of History, Vol. XVII, Number 4*, New York, June, 1966

Webb, James R., "The Fateful Encounter: Burr vs. Hamilton on the Weehawken Heights,"*American Heritage: The Magazine of History, Vol. XXVI, Number 5*, New York, August, 1975

Weisberger, Bernard A. (Chief Consultant), Foner, Eric (Ph.D), Greene, Jack P (Ph.D), Miller, Zane (Ph.D), Nugent, Walter (Ph.D), Williams, T. Harry (Ph.D), *The Reader's Digest Family Encyclopedia of American History*, The Reader's Digest Association, Inc., Pleasantville, NY, 1975

Westhorp, Christopher & Collins, Richard, *Pocket Guide to Native Americans,* Crescent Books, Avenel, NJ, 1993, 0-517-08653-0

Whitcomb, John & Claire, *Oh Say Can You See: Unexpected Anecdotes about American History*, Quill/William Morrow, New York, 1987, 0-688-08664-0

Sources for Historical Illustrations and Photographs:

http://ushistoryimages.com, Hatzigeorgiou, Karen J. U.S. History Images. 2009

http://commons.wikimedia.org

http://free-stock-photos.com

Yearly Positions of Eris—1700-2050

The degree given for each year is usually as of January, although in the later years when Eris moved much more slowly, and often retrograde, we have given the dominant degree for the year—the one accurate for the majority of months. Each year of Eris' ingress into a new sign is indicated by month and year in bold type to show the change, even though her retrograde motion often took her back into the prior sign for part of the following year or two.

1700 12 Libra	1738 28 Scorpio	1774 5 Capricorn
1701 14 Libra	**1739, Jan. 0 Sagittarius**	1775 6 Capricorn
1702 15 Libra	1739 0 Sagittarius	1776 7 Capricorn
1703 17 Libra	1740 1 Sagittarius	1777 8 Capricorn
1704 18 Librai	1741 2 Sagittarius	1778 9 Capricorn
1705 19 Libra	1742 3 Sagittarius	1779 10 Capricorn
1706 21 Libra	1743 4 Sagittarius	1780 11 Capricorn
1707 22 Libra	1744 5 Sagittarius	1781 12 Capricorn
1708 23 Libra	1745 6 Sagittarius	1782 13 Capricorn
1709 25 Libra	1746 7 Sagittarius	1783 14 Capricorn
1710 26 Libra	1747 8 Sagittarius	1784 15 Capricorn
1711 27 Libra	1748 9 Sagittarius	1785 16 Capricorn
1712 29 Libra	1749 10 Sagittarius	1786 17 Capricorn
1713, Jan. 0 Scorpio	1750 11 Sagittarius	1787 17 Capricorn
1714 1 Scorpio	1751 12 Sagittarius	1788 18 Capricorn
1715 2 Scorpio	1752 13 Sagittarius	1789 19 Capricorn
1716 4 Scorpio	1753 14 Sagittarius	1790 20 Capricorn
1717 5 Scorpio	1754 15 Sagittarius	1791 21 Capricorn
1718 6 Scorpio	1755 16 Sagittarius	1792 22 Capricorn
1719 7 Scorpio	1756 17 Sagittarius	1793 23 Capricorn
1720 8 Scorpio	1757 18 Sagittarius	1794 24 Capricorn
1721 9 Scorpio	1758 19 Sagittarius	1795 24 Capricorn
1722 11 Scorpio	1759 20 Sagittarius	1796 25 Capricorn
1723 12 Scorpio	1760 22 Sagittarius	1797 26 Capricorn
1724 13 Scorpio	1761 23 Sagittarius	1798 27 Capricorn
1725 14 Scorpio	1762 24 Sagittarius	1799 28 Capricorn
1726 15 Scorpio	1763 25 Sagittarius	1800 28 Capricorn
1727 16 Scorpio	1764 26 Sagittarius	**1800, Mar. 0 Aquarius**
1728 17 Scorpio	1765 27 Sagittarius	1801 29 Capricorn
1729 19 Scorpio	1766 28 Sagittarius	1802 0 Aquarius
1730 20 Scorpio	1767 29 Sagittarius	1803 1 Aquarius
1731 21 Scorpio	**3/1767 0 Capricorn**	1804 2 Aquarius
1732 22 Scorpio	1768 0 Capricorn	1805 3 Aquarius
1733 23 Scorpio	1769 1 Capricorn	1806 3 Aquarius
1734 24 Scorpio	1770 2 Capricorn	1807 4 Aquarius
1735 25 Scorpio	1771 3 Capricorn	1808 5 Aquarius
1736 26 Scorpio	1772 3 Capricorn	1809 6 Aquarius
1737 27 Scorpio	1773 4 Capricorn	1810 6 Aquarius

Yearly Positions for Eris —1700-2050

1811	7 Aquarius	1853	2 Pisces	1896	20 Pisces
1812	8 Aquarius	1854	3 Piscesi	1897	20 Pisces
1813	8 Aquarius	1855	3 Pisces	1898	21 Pisces
1814	9 Aquarius	1856	4 Pisces	1899	21 Pisces
1815	10 Aquarius	1857	4 Pisces	1900	21 Pisces
1816	11 Aquarius	1858	5 Pisces	1901	22 Pisces
1817	11 Aquarius	1859	5 Pisces	1902	22 Pisces
1818	12 Aquarius	1860	6 Pisces	1903	22 Pisces
1819	13 Aquarius	1861	6 Pisces	1904	23 Pisces
1820	13 Aquarius	1862	7 Pisces	1905	23 Pisces
1821	14 Aquarius	1863	7 Pisces	1906	23 Pisces
1822	15 Aquarius	1864	8 Pisces	1907	24 Pisces
1823	15 Aquarius	1865	8 Pisces	1908	24 Pisces
1824	16 Aquarius	1866	8 Pisces	1909	24 Pisces
1825	17 Aquarius	1867	9 Pisces	1910	25 Pisces
1826	17 Aquarius	1868	9 Pisces	1911	25 Pisces
1827	18 Aquarius	1869	10 Pisces	1912	25 Pisces
1828	19 Aquarius	1870	10 Pisces	1913	25 Pisces
1829	19 Aquarius	1871	11 Pisces	1914	26 Pisces
1830	20 Aquarius	1872	11 Pisces	1915	26 Pisces
1831	20 Aquarius	1873	11 Pisces	1916	26 Pisces
1832	21 Aquarius	1874	12 Pisces	1917	27 Pisces
1833	22 Aquarius	1875	12 Pisces	1918	27 Pisces
1834	22 Aquarius	1876	12 Pisces	1919	27 Pisces
1835	23 Aquarius	1877	13 Pisces	1920	28 Pisces
1836	23 Aquarius	1878	13 Pisces	1921	28 Pisces
1837	24 Aquarius	1879	14 Pisces	1922	28 Pisces
1838	25 Aquarius	1880	14 Pisces	1923	29 Pisces
1839	25 Aquarius	1881	15Pisces	1924	29 Pisces
1840	26 Aquarius	1882	15 Pisces		
1841	26 Aquarius	1883	15 Pisces	**1924, Apr. 0 Aries**	
1842	27 Aquarius	1884	16 Pisces	1925	29 Pisces
1843	27 Aquarius	1885	16 Pisces	1926	29 Pisces
1844	28 Aquarius	1886	16 Pisces	1927	0 Aries
1845	28 Aquarius	1887	17 Pisces	1928	0 Aries
1846	29 Aquarius	1888	17 Pisces	1929	0 Aries
1847	29 Aquarius	1889	17 Pisces	1930	1 Aries
		1890	18 Pisces	1931	1 Aries
1847, Feb. 0 Pisces		1891	18 Pisces	1932	1 Aries
1848	0 Pisces	1892	19 Pisces	1933	1 Aries
1849	0 Pisces	1893	19 Pisces	1934	2 Aries
1850	1 Pisces	1894	19 Pisces	1935	2 Aries
1851	1 Pisces	1895	20 Pisces	1936	2 Aries
1852	2 Pisces				

Yearly Positions for Eris —1700-2050

1937	2 Aries	1980	13 Aries	2023	24 Aries
1938	3 Aries	1981	14 Aries	2024	24 Aries
1939	3 Aries	1982	14 Aries	2025	24 Aries
1940	3 Aries	1983	14 Aries	2026	25 Aries
1941	4 Aries	1984	14 Aries	2027	25 Aries
1942	4 Aries	1985	15 Aries	2028	25 Aries
1943	4 Aries	1986	15 Aries	2029	26 Aries
1944	4 Aries	1987	15 Aries	2030	26 Aries
1945	5 Aries	1988	15 Aries	2031	26 Aries
1946	5 Aries	1989	16 Aries	2032	26 Aries
1947	5 Aries	1990	16 Aries	2033	26 Aries
1948	5 Aries	1991	16 Aries	2034	26 Aries
1949	6 Aries	1992	16 Aries	2035	27 Aries
1950	6 Aries	1993	17 Aries	2036	27 Aries
1951	6 Aries	1994	17 Aries	2037	27 Aries
1952	6 Aries	1995	17 Aries	2038	27 Aries
1953	7 Aries	1996	17 Aries	2039	27 Aries
1954	7 Aries	1997	18 Aries	2040	28 Aries
1955	7 Aries	1998	18 Aries	2041	28 Aries
1956	8 Aries	1999	18 Aries	2042	28Aries
1957	8 Aries	2000	18 Aries	2043	28 Aries
1958	8 Aries	2001	19 Aries	2044	29 Aries
1959	8 Aries	2002	19 Aries	**2044, July 0 Taurus**	
1960	9 Aries	2003	19 Aries	2045	29 Aries
1961	9 Aries	2004	19 Aries	2046	29 Aries
1962	9 Aries	2005	20 Aries	2047	29 Aries
1963	9 Aries	2006	20 Aries	2048	0 Taurus
1964	10 Aries	2007	20 Aries	2049	0 Taurus
1965	10 Aries	2008	21 Aries	2050	0 Taurus
1966	10 Aries	2009	21 Aries		
1967	10 Aries	2010	21 Aries		
1968	11 Aries	2011	21 Aries		
1969	11 Aries	2012	21 Aries		
1970	11 Aries	2013	22 Aries		
1971	11 Aries	2014	22 Aries		
1972	12 Aries	2015	22 Aries		
1973	12 Aries	2016	22 Aries		
1974	12 Aries	2017	22 Aries		
1975	12 Aries	2018	23 Aries		
1976	12 Aries	2019	23 Aries		
1977	13 Aries	2020	23 Aries		
1978	13 Aries	2021	23 Aries		
1979	13 Aries	2022	24 Aries		

Index

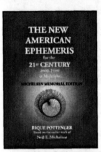
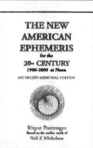

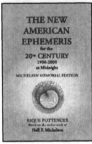
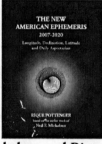

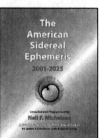
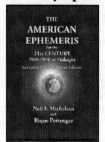

Also from Starcrafts LLC
Imprints: *Starcrafts Publishing, ACS Publications*

All About Astrology, a series of booklets by various authors
The American Atlas, Expanded 5th Edition, Thomas G. Shanks
The American Ephemeris for the 21st Century [at Noon or at Midnight]
2000-2050, *Rev. & Exp. 3rd Ed.*, Neil F. Michelsen, Revisions by Rique Pottenger
The American Heliocentric Ephemeris 2001-2050, Neil F. Michelsen
The American Sidereal Ephemeris 2001-2025, Neil F. Michelsen
The Asteroid Ephemeris 1900-2050, Rique Pottenger with Neil F. Michelsen
Astrological Alchemy, Joan Negus
Astrology for the Light Side of the Brain, Kim Rogers-Gallagher
Astrology for the Light Side of the Future, Kim Rogers-Gallagher
Astrology: the Next Step, Maritha Pottenger
Astrology and Weight Control, Beverly Ann Flynn
The Book of Jupiter, Marilyn Waram
Dial Detective, Revised Second Edition, Maria Kay Simms
Easy Astrology Guide, Maritha Pottenger
Easy Tarot Guide, Marcia Masino
Future Signs, Maria Kay Simms
The International Atlas, Revised 6th Edition,
Thomas G. Shanks & Rique Pottenger
The Michelsen Book of Tables, Neil F. Michelsen
Moon Tides, Soul Passages, Maria Kay Simms,
with software CD by Rique Pottenger
The New American Ephemeris for the 20th Century, 1900-2000, at Midnight
Michelsen Memorial Edition, Rique Pottenger, based on Michelsen
The New American Ephemeris for the 20th Century, 1900-2000, at Noon
Michelsen Memorial Edition, Rique Pottenger, based on Michelsen
The New American Ephemeris for the 21st Century, 2000-2100 at Midnight
Michelsen Memorial Edition, Rique Pottenger, based on Michelsen
The New American Ephemeris for the 21st Century, 2007-2020:
Longitude, Declination, Latitude & Daily Aspectarian,
Rique Pottenger, based on Michelsen
The New American Midpoint Ephemeris 2007-2020,
Rique Pottenger, based on Michelsen
The Only Way to Learn Astrology, Vols. 1-6 series
Marion D. March & Joan McEvers
Past Lives, Future Choices, Maritha Pottenger
Pathways to Success, Gayle Geffner
Planetary Heredity, Michel Gauquelin
Planets on the Move, Maritha Pottenger and Zipporah Dobyns, Ph.D.
Psychology of the Planets, Francoise Gauquelin
Tables of Planetary Phenomena, Third Edition, Neil F. Michelsen
Unveiling Your Future, Maritha Pottenger and Zipporah Dobyns, Ph.D.
Your Magical Child, Maria Kay Simms
Your Starway to Love, Maritha Pottenger
Zodiac Gift Guide, Carol Sandy

CPSIA information can be obtained at www.ICGtesting.com
Printed in the USA
LVOW07s1120221115

463662LV00017B/388/P

9 781934 976234